Coll
ge

MA
CHINESE
PHRASEBOOK
& DICTIONARY

Published by Collins
An imprint of HarperCollins Publishers
Westerhill Road
Bishopbriggs
Glasgow G64 2QT

Third Edition 2017

10 9 8 7 6 5 4 3 2 1

© HarperCollins Publishers 2007, 2010, 2017

ISBN 978-0-00-813590-4

Collins® and Collins Gem®
are registered trademarks of
HarperCollins Publishers Limited

www.collinsdictionary.com

Typeset by Davidson Publishing
Solutions, Glasgow

Printed and bound in China by
RR Donnelley APS

If you would like to comment on any
aspect of this book, please contact us
at the given address or online.
E-mail: dictionaries@harpercollins.co.uk
🅕 facebook.com/collinsdictionary
🐦 @collinsdict

Acknowledgements

We would like to thank those authors
and publishers who kindly gave
permission for copyright material to be
used in the Collins Corpus. We would
also like to thank Times Newspapers Ltd
for providing valuable data.

Editor

Holly Tarbet

Contributors

Julie Kleeman
Lin Luan
Ling Song Chase

For the Publisher

Gerry Breslin
Janice McNeillie

Front cover image:
Shanghai skyline with reflection, China.
© chuyuss / Shutterstock.com

Using your phrasebook

Whether you're on holiday or on business, your **Collins Gem Phrasebook and Dictionary** is designed to help you locate the exact phrase you need, when you need it. You'll also gain the confidence to go beyond what is in the book, as you can adapt the phrases by using the dictionary section to substitute your own words.

The **Gem Phrasebook and Dictionary** includes:
- Over 60 topics arranged thematically, so that you can easily find an expression to suit the situation

- Pinyin pronunciation which accompanies each word and phrase, to make sure you are understood when speaking aloud

- Tips to safeguard against any cultural faux pas, providing the essential dos and don'ts of local customs or etiquette

- A basic grammar section which will help you to build on your phrases

- **FACE TO FACE** dialogue sections to give you a flavour of what to expect from a real conversation

- **YOU MAY HEAR** sections for common announcements and messages, so that you don't miss important information when out and about

- A dictionary with over 1,000 words and their translations, to ensure you'll never be stuck for something to say

- **LIFELINE** phrases listed on the inside covers for quick reference. These basic words and phrases will be essential to your time abroad

Before you jet off, it's worth spending time looking through the topics to see what is covered and becoming familiar with pronunciation.

The colour key below shows you how to search the phrasebook by theme, so you'll be able to find relevant phrases very quickly.

Talking to people

Getting around

Staying somewhere

Shopping

Leisure

Communications

Practicalities

Health

Eating out

Menu reader

Reference

Grammar

Dictionary

Contents

Pronouncing Mandarin

• •

It is not easy for foreigners to pronounce Mandarin
Chinese, so in this phrasebook we have used
standard Latin phonetic sounds to keep it simple.
Mandarin is not written using an alphabet, but by
various strokes (such as 一, 丨). Written Chinese
is based on these 'characters' rather than words.
The standard Mandarin Chinese pronunciation
system (called 'pinyin') is based on consonants
and vowels which look just like English words.
By converting a pinyin character (each representing
the sound of the Chinese character) into the
standard Latin phonetic sound, English/European
language speakers will be able to pronounce
pinyin easily.

The system of conversion is as follows:

Consonants		
Pinyin	Phonetic sound	Converting example
b, d, f, g, j, l, m, n, p, s, t, w, y	pronounced the same as in English	bǎo→bao (宝, treasure)

Consonants

Pinyin	Phonetic sound	Converting example
c	similar to *ts* in *boots*	cí→tsi (词, word/s)
h	similar to *ch* in Scottish *loch*	hē→he (喝, to drink)
q	similar to *ch* in *chip*	qīng→ching (清, clear)
r	similar to *r* in *red*	rén→ren (人, person/people)
x	similar to *sh* in *she*	xī→she (西, west)
z	like *ds* in *kids*	zāi→dsai (灾, disaster)
zh	like *j* in *joke*	zhōng→jong (中, middle)

Vowels

Pinyin	Phonetic sound	Converting example
a	like *a* in *Zara*	mā→ma (妈, mum)
e	like *e* in *her* without the sound of *r*	hē→he (喝, to drink)
i	like *ee* in *bee*	mǐ→mi (米, rice)
o	like the sound of *war*	wǒ→war (我, I/me)
u	like *oo* in *spoon*	lù→loo (路, road)
ü	like the sound of letter *u*, followed by *ee* in *bee*	ǜ→chu–ee (去, to go)
ai	like the sound of *I*	ài→I (爱, love)
ei	like the sound of letter *a*	měi→may (美, beautiful)
ao	like *ou* in *ouch*	lǎo→lou (老, old)

Intonation

There are five tones used when pronouncing Mandarin; to make it easier for you to remember them, we have placed the diacritics on top of the vowel in each pinyin to indicate the flat tone (ˉ), the rising tone (ˊ), the musical long tone (ˇ), the strong tone (ˋ), whilst no diacritic means a quiet tone.

In order to make it easier for you to understand these tones, the following examples are supplied. These will give you some idea of how to pronounce the four basic tones in Mandarin:

Mandarin pinyin	English sounds
mā	pronounced like 'ma' in the first syllable of 'marmalade'
má	pronounced like 'ma' in 'mass' but with a slightly rising tone
mǎ	pronounced like 'mar' in 'marquee' but holding this sound for slightly longer
mà	pronounced like 'mar' in the first syllable of 'marmalade'

Top ten tips

. . . .

1 Chinese people show great respect for the wisdom
   and experience of their elders. The senior people
   present will usually initiate the greetings, and
   you should greet the oldest, most senior person
   before any others.

2 Do not stick your chopsticks into a bowl of rice.
   It reminds Chinese people of the incense sticks
   they burn when they bury their dead.

3 Avoid sharing a pear with loved ones. The word
   for pear-sharing sounds the same as the term for
   to separate (fēn-lí), and can hint at a break-up or
   a lifelong separation.

4 Business cards should be held in both hands when
   they are being offered or received. When receiving
   another person's card, you should take the time
   to look at it attentively before putting it away.

5 Be aware of the Chinese fear of losing face.
   For example, do not call a restaurant manager
   a fú-wù-yuán (waiter/waitress), or anything else
   below their true status.

6 It is rude to refuse any consumable item being offered to you (including cigarettes). If you do not accept a cigarette you have to come up with a good reason to avoid offending anyone!

7 Tipping is still not expected in most restaurants and hotels, however attitudes towards tipping are changing.

8 Most Chinese women continue using their maiden names even after marriage, but they may indicate their marital status by using 太太 (tài-tai) or 夫人 (fū-rén) with their husband's name.

9 In a formal situation you should always exchange business cards and shake hands with the most important person first and then work down, to avoid anyone losing face.

10 Whistling and pointing with the index finger are taboo gestures in China.

Talking to people

Hello/goodbye, yes/no

It is very important to use the appropriate form of greeting in China. As with other cultures, the way that you greet somebody will depend on whether you know them or if they are a stranger. The most common greeting which can be used at any time, to anyone, is 你好 (nǐ hǎo).

The form 您好 (nín hǎo) is more formal and should be used when you want to show particular respect.

Please	请 qǐng
Thanks (very much)	(多)谢 (duō)-xiè
You're welcome!	不客气！ bù kè-qì!

13

Yes	是	shì
No	不是	bù-shì
Yes, please	好, 谢谢	hǎo, xiè-xie
No, thanks	不, 谢谢	bù, xiè-xie
OK!	好!	hǎo!
Sir/Mr...	···先生	...xiān-sheng
Madam/Ms...	···女士	...nǚ-shì
Mrs...	···太太	...tài-tai
Miss...	···小姐	...xiǎo- jiě

Hello	你好	nǐ-hǎo
Hi!	嗨！	hēi!
Hello! (usually on the phone)	喂！	wèi!
Goodbye	再见	zài-jiàn
See you later	一会儿见	yī-huìr jiàn
Bye!	再会！	zài-huì!
See you at seven	7点见	qī-diǎn jiàn
See you on Monday!	星期一见！	xīng-qī-yī jiàn!
Good morning!	早上好！	zǎo-shang hǎo!

Morning!	早!	zǎo!
Good evening/ Goodnight	晚安	wǎn ān
See you tomorrow	明天见	míng-tiān jiàn
Excuse me!/ Sorry!	对不起!	duì-bù-qǐ!
Excuse me! (to get past in a crowd)	请让一让!	qǐng ràng-yī-ràng!
How are you?	你好吗?	nǐ hǎo ma?
How have you been?	最近身体怎么样?	zuì-jìn shēn-tǐ zěn-me-yàng?
Fine, thanks	很好, 谢谢	hěn hǎo, xiè-xie
Great!	棒极了!	bàng jí le!

So-so	一般 yī-bān
And you?	你呢? nǐ ne?
Long time no see!	好久不见! hǎo-jiǔ bù jiàn!
How are you doing?	最近还好吗? zuì-jìn hái hǎo ma?
I don't understand	我不明白 wǒ bù míng-bai
I don't speak Mandarin	我不会说普通话 wǒ bù huì shuō pǔ-tōng-huà

Key phrases

. . . .

| Do you have a room? | 你们有客房吗?
nǐ-men yǒu kè-fáng ma? |
| Do you have milk? | 你们有牛奶吗?
nǐ-men yǒu niú-nǎi ma? |

I'd like...	我想… wǒ xiǎng...
We'd like...	我们想… wǒ-men xiǎng...
I'd like an ice cream	我想买一个冰淇淋 wǒ xiǎng mǎi yī-gè bīng-qí-lín
We'd like to go home	我们想回家 wǒ-men xiǎng huí-jiā
Another/ Some more...	另外的/更多的 lìng-wài-de/gèng-duō-de...
How much is it?/ How much does it cost?	多少钱? duō-shǎo qián?
large	大 dà
small	小 xiǎo
with/without	有/没有 yǒu/méi-yǒu

| Where is...?/ | …在哪儿? |
| Where are...? | …zāi nǎr? |

| the nearest | 离这儿最近的 |
| | lí zhèr zuì-jìn-de |

| How do I get...? | 我怎么去…? |
| | wǒ zěn-me qù...? |

| to the museum | 去博物馆 |
| | qù bó-wù-guǎn |

| to the station | 去车站 |
| | qù chē-zhàn |

| to Shanghai | 去上海 |
| | qù shàng-hǎi |

| There is.../ | 有… |
| There are... | yǒu… |

There isn't.../	没有…
There aren't	méi-yǒu…
any...	

| When? | 什么时候? |
| | shén-me shí-hou? |

At what time...?	什么时间…? shén-me shí-jiān...?
today	今天 jīn-tiān
tomorrow	明天 míng-tiān
Can I...?	我能 … 吗? wǒ néng … ma?
smoke	抽烟 chōu-yān
taste it	尝尝它 cháng-chang tā
How does this work?	如何使用? rú-hé shǐ-yòng?
What does this mean?	这是什么意思? zhè-shì shén-me yì-sī?

Celebrations

I'd like to wish you... | 我祝愿您…
wǒ zhù-yuàn nín...

Happy Birthday! | 生日快乐!
shēng-rì kuài-lè!

Happy Anniversary! | 纪念日快乐!
jì-niàn-rì kuài-lè!

Merry Christmas! | 圣诞快乐!
shèng-dàn kuài-lè!

Happy New Year! | 新年快乐!
xīn-nián kuài-lè!

Happy Easter! | 复活节快乐!
fù-huó-jié kuài-lè!

Have a good trip! | 一路顺风!
yī-lù-shùn-fēng!

Making friends

Chinese family names are placed first, followed by the given name. For instance, in the name 'Zhao Li,' 'Zhao' is the family name, 'Li' the given name. Family names usually consist of one character, whereas given names can have either one or two characters.

Chinese people call their close friends and family members by their given names.

For example, 'Ma Wenli' may be addressed by close friends as 'Wenli.'

FACE TO FACE

你叫什么名字?
nǐ jiào shén-me míng-zi?
What's your name?

我叫···
wǒ jiào...
My name is...

你是哪里人?
nǐ shì nǎ-li rén?
Where are you from?

我是英国人, 我来自伦敦
wǒ shì yīng-guó-rén, wǒ lái zì lún-dūn
I am English, from London

很高兴认识你!
hěn gāo-xìng rèn-shi nǐ!
Pleased to meet you!

How old are you? 你多大了?
nǐ duō-dà le?

I'm ... years old 我 ··· 岁了
wǒ ... suì le

England/English 英格兰/英格兰的
yīng-gé-lán/yīng-gé-lán de

Scotland/Scottish 苏格兰/苏格兰的
sū-gé-lán/sū-gé-lán de

Wales/Welsh 威尔士/威尔士的
wēi-ěr-shì/wēi-ěr-shì de

Ireland/Irish 爱尔兰/爱尔兰的
ài-ěr-lán/ài-ěr-lán de

23

| USA/American | 美国/美国的 |
| | měi-guó/měi-guó de |

| Australia/ Australian | 澳大利亚/澳大利亚的 |
| | ào-dà-lì-yà/ào-dà-lì-yà de |

| Where do you live? | 你住在哪儿? |
| | nǐ zhù-zài nǎr? |

| Where do you live? (plural) | 你们住在哪儿? |
| | nǐ-men zhù-zài nǎr? |

| I live in London | 我住在伦敦 |
| | wǒ zhù-zài lún-dūn |

| We live in Glasgow | 我们住在格拉斯哥 |
| | wǒ-men zhù-zài gé-lā-sī-gē |

| I'm at school | 我在上学 |
| | wǒ zài shàng-xué |

| I work | 我在工作 |
| | wǒ zài gōng-zuò |

| I'm retired | 我退休了 |
| | wǒ tuì-xiū le |

| I'm... | 我… |
| | wǒ... |

| single | 单身 |
| | dān-shēn |

| married | 结婚了 |
| | jié-hūn le |

| divorced | 离婚了 |
| | lí-hūn le |

| I have... | 我有… |
| | wǒ yǒu... |

| a boyfriend | 一位男朋友 |
| | yī-wèi nán-péng-you |

| a girlfriend | 一位女朋友 |
| | yī-wèi nǚ-péng-you |

| a partner | 一位伴侣 |
| | yī-wèi bàn-lǚ |

| I have...
children | 我有 … 孩子 |
| | wǒ yǒu ... hái-zi |

I have no children	我没有孩子 wǒ méi-yǒu hái-zi
Let me introduce you to my friends	让我把你介绍给我的朋友们 ràng wǒ bǎ nǐ jiè-shào gěi wǒ de péng-you-men
I'd like you to meet my husband	我想让你认识一下我的丈夫 wǒ xiǎng ràng nǐ rèn-shi yī-xià wǒ de zhàng-fu
This is Janet	这是珍妮特 zhè shì Zhēn-ní-tè
I'm here...	我在这里… wǒ zà zhè-lǐ...
on holiday	度假 dù-jià
on business	公务 gōng-wù
for the weekend	过周末 guò zhōu-mò

Work

In formal situations you should address Chinese people by their family name or full name and the appropriate courtesy title. Unlike English, professional, social, and family titles always follow the name.

Mr Liu	刘先生	Liú xiān-sheng
Mr Li Nan	李楠先生	Lǐ Nán xiān-sheng
Mrs Liu	刘夫人	Liú fū-rén
Miss Liu	刘小姐	Liú xiǎo-jiě
Ms Liu	刘女士	Liú nǔ-shì
Dr Ma	马医生	Mǎ yī-shēng
Professor Xu	徐教授	Xú jiào-shòu

What do you do? 你干什么工作?
nǐ gàn shén-me gōng-zuò?

Do you like
your job? 你喜欢你的工作吗?
nǐ xǐ-huan nǐ de gōng-zuò ma?

I'm... 我是···
wǒ shì...

a doctor	一名医生 yī míng yī-shēng
a manager	一名经理 yī míng jīng-lǐ
I work from home	我在家里工作 wǒ zài jiā-lǐ gōng-zuò
I'm self-employed	我是自谋职业者 wǒ shì zì-móu-zhí-yè-zhě

Weather

天气预报 tiān-qì yù-bào	weather forecast
多变的气候 duō biàn de qì-hòu	changeable weather

fine	好 hǎo
bad	坏 huài

cloudy	多云 duō-yún
It's sunny	天晴 tiān-qíng
It's raining	下雨 xià-yǔ
It's snowing	下雪 xià-xuě
It's windy	刮风 guā-fēng
What a lovely day!	天气真好! tiān-qì zhēn hǎo!
What awful weather!	天气真糟糕! tiān-qì zhēn zāo-gāo!
What will the weather be like tomorrow?	明天天气会怎么样呢? míng-tiān tiān-qì huì zén-me-yàng ne?
Do you think it's going to rain?	你认为天会下雨吗? nǐ rèn-wéi tiān huì xià-yǔ ma?

It's very hot/cold today
今天很热/冷
jīn-tiān hěn rè/lěng

Do you think there will be a storm?
你认为会刮风暴吗?
nǐ rèn-wéi huì guā-fēng-bào ma?

Do you think it will snow?
你认为会下雪吗?
nǐ rèn-wéi huì xià-xuě ma?

Will it be foggy?
会有雾吗?
huì yǒu-wù ma?

What is the temperature?
气温是多少?
qì-wēn shì duō-shǎo?

Getting around

Asking the way

If you want to attract the attention of someone you do not know – for example, in the street – you say 请问 (qǐng-wèn).

对面的	duì-miàn-de	opposite
旁边的	páng-biān-de	next to
邻近	lín-jìn	near to
红绿灯 hóng-lǜ-dēng		traffic lights
十字路口 shí-zì-lù-kǒu		crossroads
(路)边	(lù)-biān	corner (of road)

请问, 我怎么去车站?

qǐng-wèn, wǒ zěn-me qù chē-zhàn?

Excuse me, how do I get to the station?

一直往前走, 过了寺庙就往左/右拐

yī-zhí wǎng qián zǒu, guò-le sì-miào jiù wǎng zuǒ/yòu guǎi

Keep straight on, after the temple turn left/right

远吗?

yuǎn ma?

Is it far?

不远, 200米/5分钟

bù yuǎn, èr-bǎi mǐ/wǔ fēn-zhōng

No, 200 metres/five minutes

谢谢您!

xiè-xie nín!

Thank you!

不客气

bù kè-qì

You're welcome

| We're lost | 我们迷路了 |
| | wǒ-men mí-lù le |

| We're looking for... | 我们正在找… |
| | wǒ-men zhèng-zài zhǎo… |

| Is this the right way to...? | 这是去 … 的路吗? |
| | zhè-shì qù … de-lù ma? |

| Can I/we walk there? | 我/我们可以步行去那里吗? |
| | wǒ/wǒ-men kě-yǐ bù-xíng qù nà-li ma? |

| How do I/ we get... | 我/我们怎么… |
| | wǒ / wǒ-men zěn-me… |

| to the museum? | 去博物馆? |
| | qù bó-wù-guǎn? |

| to the shops? | 去商店 |
| | qù shāng-diàn? |

| Can you show me on the map? | 你能在地图上指给我看吗? |
| | nǐ néng zài dì-tú shàng zhǐ gěi wǒ kàn ma? |

| 在那里 | zài nà-li | down there |
| 在后面 | zài hòu-miàn | behind |

Bus and coach

Buses are the most common form of short-distance travel in China. They are also great for inter-city/province travel, as there is a very advanced motorway system in China. Compared to train and plane tickets, bus tickets are cheap. In big cities like Beijing and Shanghai, there are combination travel cards, such as 一卡通 (yī-kǎ-tōng), which can be used to take buses, taxis, and on the metro.

FACE TO FACE

请问, 哪辆公共汽车去市/镇中心?
qǐng-wèn, nǎ liàng gōng-gòng-qì-chē qù shì/
zhèn zhōng-xīn?
Excuse me, which bus goes to the city/town centre?

15路汽车
shí-wǔ-lù-qì-chē
Number 15

公共汽车在哪里?
gōng-gòng-qì-chē zài nǎ-li?
Where is the bus stop?

那里, 在右边
nà-li, zài yòu-biān
There, on the right

我在哪里可以买车票?
wǒ zài nǎ-li kě-yǐ mǎi chē-piào?
Where can I buy the tickets?

在售票处
zài shòu-piào-chù
At the ticket office

Is there a bus to...?	有公共汽车去 ⋯ 吗? yǒu gōng-gòng-qì-chē qù ... ma?
Is there a tram to...?	有电车去 ⋯ 吗? yǒu diàn-chē qù ... ma?

| Where do I catch the bus to...? | 我在哪里乘搭去 ⋯ 的公共汽车? |
| | wǒ zài nǎ-lǐ chéng-dā qù-de gōng-gòng-qì-chē...? |

| Where do I catch the tram to...? | 我在哪里乘搭去 ⋯ 的电车? |
| | wǒ zài nǎ-lǐ chéng-dā qù-de diàn-chē...? |

| We're going to... | 我们正去⋯ |
| | wǒ-men zhèng qù... |

| How much is it to go...? | 去 ⋯ 要多少钱? |
| | qù ... yào duō-shǎo qián? |

| to the city/ town centre | 去市/镇中心 |
| | qù shì/zhèn zhōng-xīn |

| to the beach | 去海滩 |
| | qù hǎi-tān |

| How often are the buses to...? | 每隔多长时间就有一班 公共汽车去⋯? |
| | měi gé dūo-cháng shí-jiān jiù yǒu yī-bān gōng-gòng-qì-chē qù...? |

When is the first/the last bus to...?	去 ··· 的第一班/最后一班公共汽车是什么时间? qù ... de dì-yī-bān/zuì-hòu-yī-bān gōng-gòng-qì-chē shì shén-me shí-jiān?
Please tell me when to get off	到时候请您告诉我下车 dào shí-hòu qǐng nín gào-sù wǒ xià-chē
Please let me off	请让我下车 qǐng ràng wǒ xià-chē
This is my stop	我要在这一站下车 wǒ yào zài zhè-yī-zhàn xià-chē
coach	旅游巴士 lǚ-yóu bā-shì
shuttle bus	班车 bān-chē

你在这一站下车 nǐ zài zhè-yī-zhàn xià-chē	This is your stop
请乘坐地铁，坐地铁要快些 qǐng chéng-zuò dì-tiě, zuò dì-tiě yào kuài-xiē	Take the metro, it's quicker

Metro

There are 38 cities in China with underground systems. Beijing, Shanghai and Guangzhou have the longest underground lines in China. Security is very strict, passengers need to have their bags/suitcases scanned at the entrance. The earliest train is around 5 am, and the latest 11 pm. The fare is calculated by the distance, but considered cheap in general given the size of the cities. In big cities like Beijing and Shanghai, travel cards, such as 一卡通 (yī-kǎ-tōng), can be used.

入口 rù-kǒu	entrance
出口 chū-kǒu	way out/exit
每周/每月 měi-zhōu/měi-yuè	weekly/monthly

A 24-hour ticket 一张24个小时以内可以使用的车票

yī-zhāng èr-shí-sì gè xiǎo-shí yǐ-nèi kě-yǐ shǐ-yòng-de chē-piào

A 48-hour ticket 一张48个小时以内可以使用的车票

yī-zhāng sì-shí-bā gè xiǎo-shí yǐ-nèi kě-yǐ shǐ-yòng-de chē-piào

Where is the nearest metro? 离这儿最近的地铁站在哪里?

lí zhèr zuì-jìn-de dì-tiě-zhàn zài-nǎ-li?

How does the ticket machine work? 如何使用售票机?

rú-hé shǐ-yòng shòu-piào-jī?

| I'm going to... | 我正在去··· |
| | wǒ zhèng-zài qù... |

| Do you have a map of the metro? | 你有一张地铁图吗？ |
| | nǐ yǒu yī-zhāng dì-tiě-tú ma? |

| How do I get to...? | 我怎么去···？ |
| | wǒ zěn-mè qù...? |

| Do I have to change? | 我要换车吗？ |
| | wǒ yào huàn-chē ma? |

| What is the next stop? | 下一站是哪一站？ |
| | xià-yī-zhàn shì nǎ-yī-zhàn? |

| Excuse me! | 请让一让！ |
| | qǐng ràng-yī-ràng! |

| This is my stop | 我要在这一站下车 |
| | wǒ yào zài zhè-yī-zhàn xià-chē |

Train

• •

Trains are the most common form of long-distance travel in China. There are two ways of buying tickets: on the national website or at ticket offices in streets and stations.

There are three types of tickets: hard seat, hard bunk and soft bunk. A hard seat ticket is often cheap, about half the price of hard bunk, while a soft bunk ticket is about the same as a plane ticket.

The system is nationalised, it is called China Railway. In the last ten years, China has built over 20,000km of 250km/h High Speed Railways. There are 8 S-N and 8 E-W routes, the trains are normally called CRH-xxx. The tickets for these trains are more expensive.

站台 zhàn-tái	platform
售票处 shòu-piào-chù	ticket office
时刻表 shí-kè-biǎo	timetable

误点 wù-diǎn	delay (appears on train noticeboards)
行李暂存 xíng-li zàn-cún	left luggage
电子票 diàn-zǐ piào	e-ticket
电子预订 diàn-zǐ yù-dìng	e-reservation

FACE TO FACE

下一趟去 … 的火车是什么时间?
xià-yī-tàng qù … de huǒ-chē shì shén-me shí-jiān?
When is the next train to...?

下午五点十分
xià-wǔ wǔ-diǎn-shí-fēn
At 17.10

我想买三张票
wǒ xiǎng mǎi sān zhāng piào
I'd like 3 tickets, please

单程还是双程?
dān-chéng hái shì shuāng-chéng?
Single or return?

On trains, if a child is no taller than 1.2 metres, the ticket is free; between 1.2-1.5 metres, it's half price; over 1.5 metres, it's full price.

Where is the station?	车站在哪里? chē-zhàn zài nǎ-li?
1 ticket/2 tickets to...	一/两张去 … 的票 yī/liǎng zhāng qù … de piào
first/second class	头等/二等 tóu-děng/èr-děng
I booked online	我是在网上预订的 wǒ shì zài wǎng-shàng yù-dìng de
Is there a supplement to pay?	要付附加费吗? yào fù fù-jiā-fèi ma?
Do I have to change?	我要换车吗? wǒ yào huàn-chē ma?
Which platform does it leave from?	从哪个站台出发? cóng nǎ-gè zhàn-tái chū-fā?

Is this the train for...?	这是去 … 的火车吗? zhè shì qù … de huǒ-chē ma?
Does it stop at...?	它在 … 停吗? tā zài … tíng ma?
When does it arrive in...?	它什么时候到达…? tā shén-me shí-hòu dào-da...?
Please tell me when we get to...	到达 … 时请告诉我 dào-dá … shí qǐng gào-sù wǒ
Is there a restaurant car?	有餐车吗? yǒu cán-chē ma?
Is this seat free?	有人坐这个座位吗? yǒu rén zuò zhè-ge zuò-wèi ma?
Excuse me! (to get past)	请让一让! qǐng ràng-yī-ràng!

Taxi

• •

Chinese taxis are cheap, convenient and operate on meters. It is not advised to take a taxi in major cities at rush hour, as bad traffic can result in large bills. The basic fee is 10-15rmb for 3kms in most cities. There is no need to tip. There are taxi stands at stations, airports and major hotels but taxis can also be hailed from the roadside. There are a number of popular taxi apps in China that can be pre-booked or called for immediate use.

I want a taxi	我想叫一辆出租车 wǒ xiǎng jiào yī-liàng chū-zū-chē
Where can I get a taxi?	我在哪儿可以叫一辆出租车? wǒ zài nǎr kě-yǐ jiào yī-liàng chū-zū-chē?
Please order me a taxi	请现在为我叫一辆出租车 qǐng xiàn-zài wèi wǒ jiào yī-liàng chū-zū-chē

45

How much will it cost to go to...?	去 ⋯ 要多少钱? qù … yào duō-shǎo qián?
the station	车站 chē-zhàn
the airport	机场 jī-chǎng
this address	这个地址 zhè-gè dì-zhǐ
How much is it?	多少钱? duō-shǎo qián?
Keep the change	不用找零钱给我 bù yòng zhǎo líng-qián gěi wǒ
Sorry, I don't have any change	对不起, 我没有零钱 duì-bù-qǐ, wǒ méi-yǒu líng-qián

Boat and ferry

● ●

Boat and ferry transportation is hardly used by Chinese citizens, since the country has a vast inland territory. Most of the time, on a body of water, there will be several bridges.

How much is a ticket...?	一张去 … 的票要多少钱? yī-zhāng qù … de piào yào duō-shǎo qián?
Single/return	单程/双程 dān-chéng/shuāng-chéng
When is the last boat?	最后一班轮船是什么时间的? zuì-hòu yī-bān lún-chuán shì shén-me shí-jiān de?

Air travel

· ·

The three busiest airports in China are **Beijing**
Capital International Airport, **Shanghai** Pudong
International Airport, and **Guangzhou** Baiyun
International Airport.

Getting around

抵达 dǐ-dá	arrivals
起飞 qǐ-fēi	departures
国际的 guó-jì-de	international
国内的 guó-nèi-de	domestic
登机口 dēng-jī-kǒu	boarding gate

How do I get to the airport?	我怎么去机场? wǒ zěn-me qù jī-chǎng?
Is there a bus to the airport?	有公共汽车去机场吗? yǒu gōng-gòng-qì-chē qù jī-chǎng ma?
Where is the luggage for the flight from...?	来自 … 航班的行李在哪里? lái-zì … háng-bān-de xíng-li zài nǎ-li?

| Where can I change some money? | 我在哪里可以换钱？ |
| | wǒ zài nǎ-li kě-yǐ huàn-qián? |

| checked luggage | 托运行李 |
| | tuō-yùn xíng-li |

| hand luggage | 手提行李 |
| | shǒu-tí xíng-li |

| Where can I print my ticket? | 我可以在哪里打印我的票？ |
| | wǒ kě-yǐ zài nǎ-li dǎ-yìn wǒ de piào? |

| I have my boarding pass on my smartphone | 我的登机牌在我的智能手机上 |
| | wǒ de dēng-jī-pái zài wǒ de zhì-néng shǒu-jī shàng |

When buying plane tickets, note that children are categorised by their age: below 2 (free), between 2 and 12 (half price), then older than 12 (full price).

YOU MAY HEAR...	
请在 ⋯ 号登机口登机 qǐng zài … hào dēng-jī-kǒu dēng-jī	Boarding will take place at gate...
请迅速去 ⋯ 号登机口 qǐng xùn-sù qù … hào dēng-jī-kǒu	Go immediately to gate number...
禁止液体　jìn-zhǐ yè-tǐ	No liquids
你的行李超重了 nǐ de xíng-li chāo-zhòng le	Your luggage exceeds the maximum weight

Customs control

Visitors to the mainland of the People's Republic of China must obtain a visa from one of the Chinese diplomatic missions, unless they come from one of the visa exempt countries. ID is essential when travelling, you need it to buy train/plane tickets and book hotels.

It is sometimes possible to spend up to three days in China as a stop-over without acquiring a visa. This suits those in transit only, as the visitor is not permitted to leave the city in which they've entered China.

| 护照 | hù-zhào | passport(s) |
| 海关 | hǎi-guān | customs |

Do I have to pay duty on this?	我要支付这商品的关税吗?	wǒ yào zhī-fù zhè shāng-pǐn de guān-shuì ma?
It's for my own personal use/ for a present	这是我自用的/送人的礼品	zhè shì wǒ zì-yòng-de/ sòng-rén-de lǐ-pǐn
We are on our way to... (if in transit through the country)	我们正在转机去…	wǒ-men zhèng-zài zhuǎn-jī qù…

Driving

• •

Car hire is not permissible in China without a Chinese driving licence. For foreign visitors, you cannot drive, but you may be travelling as a passenger with a Chinese friend.

4星　sì-xīng	4 star
柴油　chái-yóu	diesel
无铅汽油 wú-qián-qì-yóu	unleaded

I want to hire a car for ... days	我想租一辆车 … 天 wǒ xiǎng zū yī-liàng chē … tiān
with automatic gears	自动档 zì-dòng-dǎng

The speed limits in China are 40 km/hr in built-up areas, 100 km/hr on main roads, and 120 km/hr on motorways.

| Can I/we park here? | 我/我们可以在这里停放车吗? |
| | wǒ/wǒ-men kě-yǐ zài zhè-lǐ tíng-fàng chē ma? |

| Which junction is it for...? | 去 … 是哪一个出口? |
| | qù … shì nǎ yī-gè chū-kǒu? |

A garage that does repairs is known as a 修车行 (xiū-chē-háng). In China there are no private companies who deal with breakdowns. You need to call the traffic police if you are on a motorway. If you are on the road in or near a city, you call the 4S shops (found in all major cities.) 4S means Sale, Spare part, Service and Survey.

| I've run out of petrol | 我没汽油了 |
| | wǒ méi qì-yóu le |

| Can you tow me to the nearest garage? | 你能把我的车拖到离这儿最近的修车行吗? |
| | nǐ néng bǎ wǒ-de chē tuō-dào lí zhèr zuì-jìn-de xiū-chē-háng ma? |

checkpoint

customs

toll booth

stop

no parking

give way

northbound

southbound

eastbound

westbound

school

food and drink

hospital

Staying somewhere

Hotel (booking)

• •

Hotel chains are popular for business trips, as they are often located in business districts with good public transport links. Those on holiday tend to stay in B&Bs or boutique hotels, as they are tastefully decorated and are close to tourist attractions.

single room 单人房
dān-rén-fáng

double room 双人房
shuāng-rén-fáng

private facilities 私人设施
sī-rén-shè-shī

number of adults 多少大人
duō-shǎo dà-rén

number of children	多少小孩 duō-shǎo xiǎo-hái

FACE TO FACE

我想预定一间单人房
wǒ xiǎng yù-dìng yī-jiān dān-rén-fáng
I'd like to book a single room

我想预定一间双人房
wǒ xiǎng yù-dìng yī-jiān shuāng-rén-fáng
I'd like to book a double room

几个晚上?
jǐ-gè wǎn-shàng?
For how many nights?

一个晚上
yī gè wǎn-shàng
for one night

从 … 开始住 … 个晚上
cóng … kāi-shǐ zhù … gè wǎn-shàng
… nights from …

直至…
zhí-zhì…
till…

How much is it per night?	每晚多少钱? měi wǎn duō-shǎo qián?
How much is it per week?	每周多少钱? měi zhōu duō-shǎo qián?
Do you have a room for tonight?	你们这里今晚还有一间客房吗? nǐ-men zhě-li jīn-wǎn hái-yǒu yī-jiān kè-fáng ma?
with bath	有浴缸 yǒu yù-gāng
with shower	有淋浴 yǒu lín-yù
with a double bed	有双人床 yǒu shuāng-rén-chuáng
twin-bedded	两张单人床 liǎng-zhāng dān-rén-chuáng
with an extra bed for a child	额外的一张小孩床 é-wài-de yī-zhāng xiǎo-hái-chuáng

Is breakfast included?	早餐包括在内吗?
	zǎo-cān bāo-kuò zài-nèi ma?
Have you got anything cheaper?	你们有其它便宜一些的客房吗?
	nǐ-men yǒu qí-tā pián—yi yī-xiē-de kè-fáng ma?
I'd like to see the room	我想看看房间
	wǒ xiǎng kàn-kan fáng-jiān

YOU MAY HEAR...

我们这儿已经住满了客人	We're full
wǒ-men zhèr yǐ-jīng zhù-mǎn-le kè-rén	
请问你叫什么名字?	Your name please
qǐng wèn nǐ jiào shén-me míng-zì?	
请用电子邮件确认	Please confirm by e-mail
qǐng yòng diàn-zǐ-yóu-jiàn què-rèn	
电话（预订）	(booking) by phone
diàn-huà (yù-dìng)	

Hotel desk

• •

Many hotels are now signposted in towns. The Chinese word for a hotel is 旅馆 (lǔ-guǎn).

I booked a room...	我已经用叫… wǒ yǐ-jīng yòng jiào…
in the name of...	的名字定了一间客房… de míng-zi dìng-le yī-jiān kè-fáng…
What time is dinner/breakfast?	几点吃晚饭/早餐? jí-diǎn chī wǎn-fàn/zǎo-cān?
The key, please	请把钥匙给我 qǐng bǎ yào-shi gěi-wǒ
Room number...	房间号码是… fáng-jiān hào-mǎ shì...
I'm leaving tomorrow	我明天离开 wǒ míng-tiān lí-kāi

I reserved the room(s) online	我在网上预订了房间 wǒ zài wǎng-shàng yù-dìng le fáng-jiān	
Does the price include breakfast?	房价包含早餐吗？ fáng-jià bāo-hán zǎo-cān ma?	
Is there a hotel restaurant/bar?	有餐厅/酒吧吗？ yǒu cān-tīng/ jiǔ-bā ma?	

Camping

. . . .

垃圾	lā-jī	rubbish
饮用水	yǐn-yòng-shuǐ	drinking water
电源	diàn-yuán	electric point

Is there a restaurant on the campsite?	在野营地有餐馆吗？ zài yě-yíng-dì yǒu cān-guǎn ma?
Do you have any vacancies?	你们这里还有客房吗？ nǐ-men zhè-li hái yǒu kè-fáng ma?

How much is it per night?	每晚多少钱? méi wǎn duō-shǎo qián?
How much is it per tent?	每个帐篷多少钱? méi-gè zhàng-péng duō-shǎo qián?
How much is it per person?	每人多少钱? měi-rén duō-shǎo qián?
Does the price include...?	价钱包括 … 吗? jià-qián bāo-kuò … ma?
showers	淋浴 lín-yù
hot water	热水 rè-shuǐ
electricity	电 diàn
We'd like to stay for ... nights	我们想住 … 个晚上 wǒ-men xiǎng zhù … gè wǎn-shàng

Self-catering

• •

The idea of a self-catering holiday is fairly uncommon for Chinese people. You will be able to find self-catering flats in big cities, if you book through companies such as Airbnb (**www.airbnb.co.uk**).

Whom do we contact if there are problems?	如果有问题我们联系谁? rú-guǒ yǒu wèn-tí wǒ-men lián-xì shuí?
How does the heating work?	暖气如何工作? nuǎn-qì rú-hé gōng-zuò?
Is there always hot water?	总有热水吗? zǒng yǒu rè-shuǐ ma?
Where is the nearest supermarket?	离这儿最近的超市在哪儿? lí zhèr zuì-jìn-de chāo-shì zài nǎr?
Where do we leave the rubbish?	我们把垃圾放在哪儿? wǒ-men bǎ lā-jī fàng zài nǎr?
recycling	回收 huí-shōu

Shopping

Shopping phrases

· · · · · · · · · · · · · · · · · · · ·

Opening hours for most shops are from 9–10 am to
9–10 pm, Monday to Sunday. The hours tend to be
longer in the summer.

FACE TO FACE

你想买什么?

nǐ xiǎng mǎi shén-me?

What would you like?

你们有 ··· 吗?

nǐ-men yǒu … ma?

Do you have...?

有,给你。你还要其它东西吗?

yǒu, gěi nǐ. nǐ hái yào qí-tā dōng-xi ma?

Certainly, here you are. Anything else?

Where is...?　　···在哪儿?

　　　　　　　···zài nǎr?

| I'm just looking | 我先看看 |
| | wǒ xiān kàn-kan |

| Where can I buy...? | 我在哪儿可以买…? |
| | wǒ zài nǎr kě-yǐ mǎi…? |

| shoes | 鞋子 |
| | xié-zi |

| gifts | 礼物 |
| | lǐ-wù |

| It's too expensive for me | 这太贵了 |
| | zhè tài guì le |

| Can you give me a discount? | 你可以给我打折吗? |
| | nǐ kě-yǐ gěi wǒ dǎ-zhé-ma? |

Shops

. . . .

| 减价 | jiǎn-jià | sale |
| 打折 | dǎ-zhé | discount |

baker's	面包店	miàn-bāo-diàn
butcher's	肉店	ròu-diàn
cake shop	蛋糕店	dàn-gāo-diàn
clothes shop	衣物店	yī-wù-diàn
fruit shop	水果店	shuǐ-guǒ-diàn
gifts	礼品店	lǐ-pǐn-diàn
grocer's	杂货店	zá-huò-diàn
hairdresser's	发廊	fà-láng
hypermarket	特大型超级市场	tè dà-xíng chāo-jí shì-chǎng
newsagent	报摊	bào-tān
optician's	眼镜店	yǎn-jìng-diàn
perfume shop	香水店	xiāng-shuǐ-diàn
pharmacy	药店	yào-diàn
photographic shop	相馆	xiàng-guǎn
shoe shop	鞋店	xié-diàn
souvenir shop	纪念品商店	jì-niàn-pǐn shāng-diàn
sports shop	运动品商店	yùn-dòng-pǐn-shāng-diàn

supermarket	超市	chāo-shì
tobacconist's	香烟店	xiāng-yān-diàn
toys	玩具	wán-jù

Supermarket

· ·

I would like to buy...	我想买…	wǒ-xiǎng-mǎi…
biscuits	饼干	bǐng-gān
bowl	碗	wǎn
bread	面包	miàn-bāo
butter	黄油	huáng-yóu
cheese	奶酪	nǎi-lào
chicken	鸡	jī
chocolate	巧克力	qiǎo-kè-lì
chopsticks	筷子	kuài-zi
coffee (instant)	速溶咖啡	sù-róng kā-fēi
cooking oil	油	yóu
cream	奶油	nǎi-yóu

crisps	薯片	shǔ-piàn
eggs	蛋	dàn
fish	鱼	yú
flour	面粉	miàn-fěn
jam	果酱	guǒ-jiàng
milk	鲜奶	xiān-nǎi
oats	麦片	mài-piàn
olive oil	橄榄油	gǎn-lǎn-yóu
pepper	胡椒粉	hú-jiāo-fěn
plate	碟子	dié-zi
rice	大米	dà-mǐ
rolling-pin	擀面棍	gǎn-miàn-gùn
salt	盐	yán
soya sauce	酱油	jiàng-yóu
spatula	锅铲	guō-chǎn
spoon	勺子	sháo-zi
sugar	糖	táng
tea	茶	chá
tomatoes (tinned)	西红柿罐头	xī-hóng-shì guàn-tóu
vinegar	醋	cù
whisk	搅拌器	jiǎo-bàn-qì

| wok | 炒菜锅 | chǎo-cài-guō |
| yoghurt | 酸奶 | suān-nǎi |

Food (fruit and veg)

Fruit 水果

apples	苹果	píng-guǒ
apricots	杏子	xìng-zi
bananas	香蕉	xiāng-jiāo
cherries	樱桃	yīng-táo
grapefruit	葡萄柚	pú-táo-yòu
grapes	葡萄	pú-táo
lemon	柠檬	níng-méng
melon	瓜	guā
oranges	橙子	chéng-zi
peaches	桃子	táo-zi
pears	雪梨	xuě-lí
plums	李子	lǐ-zi
strawberries	草莓	cǎo-méi
watermelon	西瓜	xī-guā

Vegetables 蔬菜

asparagus	芦笋	lú-sǔn
aubergine	茄子	qié-zi
carrots	胡萝卜	hú-luó-bo
cauliflower	菜花	cài-huā
celery	芹菜	qín-cài
cucumber	黄瓜	huáng-guā
garlic	大蒜	dà-suàn
mushrooms	蘑菇	mó-gu
onions	洋葱	yáng-cōng
peas	豌豆	wān-dòu
pepper	青椒	qīng-jiāo
potatoes	土豆	tǔ-dòu
salad	沙拉	shā-lā
spinach	菠菜	bō-cài
tomatoes	西红柿	xī-hóng-shì

Clothes

women's sizes		men's sizes		shoe sizes			
UK	China	UK	China	UK	China	UK	China
8	S	32	L	4	37	9	42
10	M	34	XL	5	38	10	43
12	L	36	XXL	6	39	11	44
14	L	38	XXXL	7	40	12	45
16	XL	40	XXXXL	8	41		
18	XXL						

FACE TO FACE

我可以试穿吗?

wǒ kě-yǐ shì-chuān ma?

May I try this on?

请往这边走

qǐng wǎng zhè-biān zǒu

Please come this way

你们有小/中/大码吗?

nǐ-men yǒu xiǎo/zhōng/dà mǎ ma?

Do you have a small/medium/large size?

你穿多大尺寸的衣服?

nǐ chuān duō-dà chǐ-cùn-de yī-fu?

What size (clothes) do you take?

bigger	大些	dà-xiē
smaller	小些	xiǎo-xiē
in other colours	其他颜色	qí-tā yán-sè

YOU MAY HEAR...

| 你穿多大尺码的鞋子?
nǐ chuān duō-dà chǐ-mǎ-de xié-zi? | What shoe size do you take? |
| 这种颜色我们只有这一尺寸
zhè-zhǒng yán-sè wǒ-men zhǐ-yǒu zhè-yī chǐ-cùn | In this colour we have this size only |

Clothes (articles)

blouse	女上衣	nǚ-shàng-yī
briefcase	公文包	gōng-wén-bāo
coat	大衣	dà-yī
dress	连衣裙	lián-yī-qún
handbag	手袋	shǒu-dài

jacket	夹克	jiá-kè
jumper	毛衣	máo-yī
knickers	女内裤	nǚ nèi-kù
pyjamas	睡衣	shuì-yī
shirt	衬衫	chèn-shān
shoes	鞋子	xié-zi
shorts	短裤	duǎn-kù
silk dress	真丝连衣裙	zhēn-sī lián-yī-qún
silk scarf	丝巾	sī-jīn
silk tie	真丝领带	zhēn-sī-lǐng-dài
skirt	短裙	duǎn-qún
socks	短袜	duǎn-wà
suitcase	手提箱	shǒu-tí-xiāng
suits	西装	xī-zhuāng
swimsuit	游泳衣	yóu-yǒng-yī
t-shirt	T恤衫	t-xù-shān
tights	裤袜	kù-wà
trainers	运动鞋	yùn-dòng-xié
trousers	裤子	kù-zi
underpants	内衣裤	nèi-yī-kù

Bookshop/music shop

字典	zì-diǎn	dictionary
小说	xiǎo-shuō	novel
唐诗	táng-shī	Tang poetry
光碟	guāng-dié	CD
歌曲	gē-qǔ	songs

Tang poetry refers to poetry written in or around the time of China's Tang dynasty, often considered as the Golden Age of Chinese poetry. In this time, poetry was deeply ingrained in society. Scholars were required to master poetry for civil service exams, but the art was theoretically available to everyone. This led to a large record of poetry and poets. Two of the most famous poets of the period were **Li Bai** and **Du Fu**.

| Do you have an English-Chinese dictionary? | 你们有中英文字典吗？
nǐ-men yǒu zhōng-yīng-wén zì-diǎn ma? |
| Do you have collections of Tang poetry? | 你们有唐诗集吗？
nǐ-men yǒu táng-shī-jí ma? |

Shopping

Do you have	你们有英文报纸吗?
any English	nǐ-men yǒu yīng-wén
newspapers?	bào-zhǐ ma?

Antique shop

. . . .

景泰蓝 jǐng-tài-lán	Cloisonné
明瓷器 míng-cí-qì	Ming porcelain
玉石 yù-shí	jade
兵马俑 bīng-mǎ-yǒng	terracotta
书法 shū-fǎ	calligraphy

Do you have any	你们有中国景泰蓝吗?
Chinese	nǐ-men yǒu zhōng-guó
Cloisonné?	jǐng-tài-lán ma?

Is this Ming	这是明瓷器吗?
porcelain?	zhè-shì míng-cí-qì ma?

I would like to	我想买一只玉石手镯
buy a jade	wǒ xiǎng mǎi yī-zhī yù-shí
bracelet	shǒu-zhuó

Chinese	书法
calligraphy	shū-fǎ

Maps and guides

收银台 shōu-yín-tái	kiosk
周刊杂志 zhōu-kān-zá-zhì	a weekly magazine
报纸 bào-zhǐ	newspaper
地图 dì-tú	map

Do you have a map...?
你们有 … 的地图吗？
nǐ-men yǒu … de dì-tú ma?

of the town
本镇
běn zhèn

of the region
地区
dì-qū

Can you show me where ... is on the map?
你能在地图上为我指出 … 在哪里吗？
nǐ néng zài dì-tú shàng wèi wǒ zhǐ-chū … zài nǎ-li ma?

Do you have a map of this city?	你们有本市的地图吗? nǐ-men yǒu běn-shì-de dì-tú ma?
Do you have a leaflet in English?	你们有英文版的小册子吗? nǐ-men yǒu yīng-wén-bǎn-de xiǎo-cè-zi ma?

Post office

Post offices are state-owned, so employees are considered to be civil servants. Opening hours vary between areas, generally the bigger the city is, the longer the hours are. On Beijing's busiest streets, the post offices may open from 8.30 am to 9 pm. In a more remote town, the post office will close at 5 pm, sometimes even with a lunch hour.

邮局	yóu-jú	post office
邮票	yóu-piào	stamps
挂号	guà-hào	registered
集邮者	jí-yóu-zhě	stamp collector
寄信/书	jì-xìn/shū	to send a letter/book

77

Where is the post office?	邮局在哪儿? yóu-jú zài nǎr?
Which is the counter...?	哪个柜台…? nǎ-gè guì-tái...?
for stamps	出售邮票 chū-shòu yóu-piào
for parcels	寄包裹 jì-bāo-guǒ
6 stamps for postcards...	六张寄明信片的邮票… liù-zhāng jì míng-xìn-piàn-de yóu-piào…
to Britain	寄往英国 jì-wǎng yīng-guó
to America	寄往美国 jì-wǎng měi-guó
to Australia	寄往澳大利亚 jì-wǎng ào-dà-lì-ya

How much more does it cost for recorded delivery?	挂号要另付多少钱?
	guà-hào yào lìng-fù duō-shǎo qián?

I am a stamp collector, I would like to buy the most recent stamps	我是一名集邮者,我想买最新的邮票
	wǒ-shì yī-míng jí-yóu-zhě, wǒ xiǎng mǎi zuì-xīn-de yóu-piào

Technology

存储卡 cún-chǔ-kǎ	memory card
打印 dǎ-yìn	to print
数码相机 shù-mǎ xiàng-jī	digital camera
电子香烟 diàn-zǐ xiāng-yān	e-cigarette

Do you have batteries for this camera?	你们有这部相机使用的电池吗?
	nǐ-men yǒu zhè-bù xiàng-jī shǐ-yòng-de diàn-chí ma?

| Can you repair...? | 请问能修 … 吗？ |
| | qǐng-wèn néng xiū … ma? |

| my screen | 我的屏幕 |
| | wǒ de píng-mù |

| my keypad | 我的键盘 |
| | wǒ de jiàn-pán |

| my lens | 我的镜头 |
| | wǒ de jìng-tóu |

| my charger | 我的充电器 |
| | wǒ de chōng-diàn-qì |

| I want to print my photos | 我想打印我的照片 |
| | wǒ xiǎng dǎ-yìn wǒ de zhào-piàn |

| I have it on my USB | 它在我的移动硬盘上 |
| | tā zài wǒ de yí-dòng yìng-pán shàng |

| I have it on my e-mail | 它在我的邮件里 |
| | tā zài wǒ de yóu-jiàn lǐ |

Leisure

Sightseeing and tourist office

For tourist information, **www.ctrip.com** is a reliable website to get travel information, reviews, to book train/plane tickets and make hotel reservations. It also has an option for an English language web interface.

Where is the tourist office?	游客服务处在哪儿? yóu-kè fú-wù-chù zài-năr?
What can we visit in the area?	在这个地方我们可以参观什么? zài zhè-ge dì-fang wŏ-men kĕ-yĭ cān-guān shén-me?
Have you any leaflets?	你们有传单吗? nĭ-men yŏu chuán-dān ma?
Are there any excursions?	有哪些短程旅行? yŏu nă-xiē duăn-chéng-lǚ-xíng?

We'd like to go to...	我们想去… wǒ-men xiǎng qù…
How much does it cost to get in?	入门券要多少钱? rù-mén-quàn yào duō-shǎo qián?
Are there reductions for...?	对 … 有优惠价 … 吗? duì … yǒu yōu-huì-jià … ma?
children	儿童 ér-tóng
students	学生 xué-shēng
over 60s	60岁以上的人士 liù-shí-suì yǐ-shàng-de rén-shì

Entertainment

• •

Each province may have its own website for tourist attractions and cultural events, but you can also find information on national websites, such as **www.chncpa.org** (National Centre for Performing Arts).

What is there to do in the evenings?	晚上有什么活动吗? wǎn-shàng yǒu shén-me huó-dòng ma?
Do you have a programme of events?	你们有节目单吗? nǐ-men yǒu jié-mù-dān ma?
Is there anything for children?	有什么孩子们可以参加的活动吗? yǒu shén-me hái-zi-men kě-yǐ cān-jiā-de huó-dòng ma?

At tourist attractions, if a child's height is under 1.5 metres, then the entry is half price. However, this might not be applicable during busy seasons or at the most popular places.

Nightlife

· · · · · · · · · · · · · · · · · · · ·

酒吧 jiǔ-bā	bar
音乐会 yīn-yuè huì	gig
音乐节 yīn-yuè jié	music festival

夜总会	yè-zǒng-huì	nightclub
派对	pài-duì	party
酒吧	jiǔ-bā	pub

| Where can I go clubbing? | 泡吧去哪里？
pào-bā qù nǎ-li? |

Leisure/interests

| Where can I/ we go...? | 我/我们去哪儿可以…？
wǒ/wǒ-men qù nǎr kě-yǐ…? |

| fishing | 钓鱼
diào-yú |

| walking | 步行
bù-xíng |

| Are there any good beaches near here? | 这附近有漂亮的沙滩吗？
zhè fù-jìn yǒu piào-liàng-de shā-tān ma? |

| Is there a swimming pool? | 有游泳池吗？
yǒu yóu-yǒng-chí ma? |

adventure centre	冒险乐园	mào-xiǎn lè-yuán
art gallery	画廊	huà-láng
boat hire	租船	zū-chuán
camping	露营	lù-yíng
photography	摄影	shè-yǐng
picnic area	野餐区	yě-cān qū
piercing	穿孔	chuān-kǒng
museum	博物馆	bó-wù-guǎn
tattoo	纹身	wén-shēn
theme park	主题公园	zhǔ-tí gōng-yuán
water park	水上乐园	shuǐ-shàng lè-yuán
zoo	动物园	dòng-wù-yuán

YOU MAY HEAR...

禁止游泳 jìn-zhǐ yóu-yǒng	No swimming
禁止跳水 jìn-zhǐ tiào-shuǐ	No diving

The Mid-Autumn Festival is a harvest festival held on the 15th day of the 8th month of the lunar calendar (with a full moon), which corresponds to late September/early October of the Gregorian calendar (with a full moon).

Traditionally, the festival was a time to enjoy the successful reaping of rice and wheat with food offerings made in honour of the moon. Today, it is still an occasion for outdoor reunions with friends and relatives, where you eat mooncakes (a round-shaped dessert with a crust and sweet stuffing) and watch the moon, a symbol of harmony and unity.

Music

. . . .

歌剧　gē-jù	musical production
芭蕾舞　bā-léi-wǔ	ballet
古典音乐会 gǔ-diǎn yīn-yuè-huì	classical music concert

I would like to see...	我想看··· wǒ-xiǎng-kàn...

| Are there any good concerts on? | 有正在上演的好音乐会吗？ |
| | yǒu zhèng-zài shàng-yǎn de hǎo yīn-yuè huì ma? |

| Where can I get tickets for the concert? | 我在哪儿可以购买音乐会的入场券？ |
| | wǒ zài nǎr kě-yǐ gòu-mǎi yīn-yuè-huì-de rù-chǎng-quàn? |

| Where can we hear some classical music/jazz? | 我们去哪儿可以听古典音乐/爵士乐？ |
| | wǒ-men qù nǎr kě-yǐ tīng gǔ-diǎn yīn-yuè/jué-shì-yuè? |

民歌	mín-gē	folk
嘻哈乐	xī-hā yuè	hip-hop
流行乐	liú-xíng yuè	pop
雷鬼乐	léi-guǐ yuè	reggae
摇滚乐	yáo-gǔn yuè	rock
电子乐	diàn-zǐ yuè	techno

Theatre/opera

京剧	jīng-jù	Peking/Beijing Opera
越剧	yuè-jù	Shanghai Opera
正厅前排 zhèng-tīng-qián-pái		stalls
半圆形楼座 bàn-yuán-xíng-lóu-zuò		circle
包厢	bāo-xiāng	box
座位	zuò-wèi	seat
衣帽间	yī-mào-jiān	cloakroom

What is on at the theatre?

剧院正在上演什么戏剧?
jù-yuàn zhèng-zài shàng-yǎn shén-me xì-jù?

What prices are the tickets?

戏票多少钱?
xì-piào duō-shǎo qián?

I'd like two tickets...

我想买两张票···
wǒ xiǎng mǎi liǎng-zhāng piào...

| for tonight | 今晚的
jīn-wǎn de |
| for tomorrow
night | 明晚的
míng-wǎn de |

| 你不能进去, 因为演出
已经开始了
ní bù-néng jìn-qù, yīn-wéi
yǎn-chū yǐ-jīng kāi-shǐ le | You can't go in, the
performance has
started |
| 你在中间休息时可以
进去
nǐ zài zhōng-jiān xiū-xi
shǐ kě-yǐ jìn-qù | You may enter at
the interval |

Sport

· ·

Tai chi (literally 'Supreme Ultimate Boxing') is a
Chinese martial art practiced for both its defence
training and health benefits. A multitude of
modern and traditional training forms exist,
which correspond to certain purposes. It is
practised for a variety of reasons: as competitive

wrestling in the format of pushing hands (**tui shou**), for demonstrative competitions, and for achieving greater longevity. Some training forms of **t'ai chi ch'uan** are especially known for being practised with relatively slow movements.

Where can I/ we go...?	我/我们可以去哪儿…? wǒ/wǒ-men kě-yǐ qù nǎr...?
swimming	游泳 yóu-yǒng
jogging	慢跑 màn-pǎo
skiing	滑雪 huá-xuě
Do you have to be a member?	你必须是会员吗? nǐ bì-xū shì huì-yuán ma?
How much is it per hour?	每小时多少钱? měi xiǎo-shi duō-shǎo qián?
Can we hire rackets/golf clubs?	我们可以租借 球拍/高尔夫球杆吗? wǒ-men kě-yǐ zū-jiè qiú-pāi/ gāo-ěr-fū-qiú-gǎn ma?

I want to try...	我想尝试做… wǒ xiǎng cháng-shì zuò…
I've never done this before	这是我以前从没做过的 zhè shì wǒ yǐ-qián cóng-méi zuò guò de
Where can I/we get tickets for the game?	我/我们在哪儿能买这场比赛的票? wǒ/wǒ-men zài nǎr néng mǎi zhè-chǎng bǐ-sài de piào?
I want to hire skis	我想租借滑雪板 wǒ xiǎng zū-jiè huá-xuě-bǎn

骑车	qí-chē	cycling
跳舞	tiào-wǔ	dancing
皮划艇	pí-huá-tǐng	kayaking
攀岩	pān-yán	rock climbing
滑雪	huá-xuě	snowboarding
排球	pái-qiú	volleyball
滑水	huá-shuǐ	water-skiing
冲浪	chōng-làng	windsurfing

Walking

. . . .

Leisure

| Do you know any good walks? | 你知道有理想的步行活动吗？ |
| | nǐ zhī-dào yǒu lǐ-xiǎng de bù-xíng-huó-dòng ma? |

| How many kilometres is the walk? | 这一步行活动要走多少公里？ |
| | zhè yī bù-xíng-huó-dòng yào zǒu duō-shǎo gōng-lǐ? |

| Is there a map of the walk? | 有这一步行活动的地图吗？ |
| | yǒu zhè yī bù-xíng-huó-dòng de dì-tú ma? |

| Do you have a detailed map of the area? | 你们有该地区详细的地图吗？ |
| | nǐ-men yǒu gāi-dǐ-qū xiáng-xì de dì-tú ma? |

Communications

Telephone and mobile

The international code for China is 00 86 plus the Chinese town or area code without the first 0, (so for Beijing (0)10, Guangzhou (0)20, Shanghai (0)21. If you are calling within China, you must always use the full area code, unless you're making local calls.

For mobile phones, SIM cards can be purchased at the major telecoms outlets. Proof of identity (usually a passport) is required for purchase.

When Chinese people make a phone call, they ask for the person they wish to speak to by name. It is not the Chinese caller's habit to give their own name first when making or receiving a call.

When giving telephone numbers, Chinese speakers normally read out the numbers one by one so that:

020 7900 0283 would be read:
零二零 七九零零 零二八三
líng èr líng qī jiǔ líng líng líng èr bā sān

手机　shǒu-jī	mobile
打电话　dǎ diàn-huà	make a phone call
电话号码 diàn-huà hào-mǎ	phone number
分机号码 fēn-jī hào-mǎ	extension number
市话　shì-huà	local call
长途电话 cháng-tú diàn-huà	national call
国际长途电话 guó-jì cháng-tú diàn-huà	international call
智能手机 zhì-néng shǒu-jī	smartphone
充电器　chōng-diàn-qì	charger

FACE TO FACE

你好
nǐ-hǎo
Hello

我想找 ⋯ 听电话
wǒ xiǎng zhǎo ... tīng diàn-huà
I'd like to speak to ... please

请问您是谁?
qǐng-wèn nín shì shuí?
Who's calling?

我是安琪拉
wǒ shì ān-qí-lā
It's Angela

请等一等…
qǐng děng-yī-děng…
Just a moment...

I want to make a phone call	我想打个电话 wǒ xiǎng dǎ gè diàn-huà
What is your mobile number?	请问你的手机号码? qǐng-wèn nǐ de shǒu-jī hào-mǎ?
My mobile number is...	我的手机号码是… wǒ de shǒu-jī hào-mǎ shì…
Can I speak to...?	我能找 … 听电话吗? wǒ něng zhǎo … tīng diàn-huà ma?

Sorry, I must have dialled the wrong number

对不起, 我拨错号了

duì-bu-qǐ, wǒ bō-cuò hào le

We were cut off

电话掉线了

diàn-huà diào-xiàn le

This is a very bad line

线路很不清楚

xiàn-lù hěn bù qīng-chu

I'll call back later

我一会儿再打过来

wǒ yī-huìr zài dǎ-guò-lái

This is Mr.../ Mrs...

我是 … 先生/太太

wǒ shì … xiàn-shēng/tài-tai

How do I get an outside line?

我如何拨打外线电话呢?

wǒ rú-hé bō-dǎ wài-xiàn diàn-huà ne?

Please switch off all mobile phones

请关掉所有的手机

qǐng guān-diào suǒ-yǒu de shǒu-jī

Do you have a...?

请问有 … 的 … 吗?

qǐng-wèn yǒu … de … ma?

Can I borrow your...?	可以借一下你的 … 吗？ kě-yǐ jiè yī-xià nǐ de … ma?
charger	充电器 chōng-diàn-qì
cable	充电线 chōng-diàn-xiàn
I have an e-ticket on my phone	我的手机上有一张电子票 wǒ de shǒu-jī shang yǒu yī-zhāng diàn-zǐ-piào
I need to phone a UK/US/ Australian number	我要给英国/美国/ 澳大利亚的号码打电话 wǒ yào gěi yīng-guó/měi-guó/ ào-dà-lì-yà de hào-mǎ dǎ diàn-huà

YOU MAY HEAR...

请问您是哪位? qǐng-wèn nín shì nǎ-wèi?	Who's speaking?
请问您找谁? qǐng-wèn nín zhǎo shuí?	Who would you like to speak to?

请别挂断 qǐng bié guà-duàn	Please hold (the line)
电话正占线，请过一会儿再打过来 diàn-huà zhèng zhàn-xiàn, qǐng guò yī-huìr zài dǎ-guò-lái	The line is engaged, please try later
你想留言吗? nǐ xiǎng liú-yán ma?	Do you want to leave a message?
请在听到信号后留言 qǐng zài tīng-dào xìn-hào hòu liú-yán	Leave a message after the tone

Text messaging

In China, there is not a widely-used abbreviated 'text language' like we have in English.

I will text you 我会给你发信息
wǒ huì gěi nǐ fā xìn-xī

Can you text me? 你能发送信息给我吗?
nǐ néng fā-sòng xìn-xī gěi-wǒ ma?

text (message)	短信
	duǎn-xìn

to text	发短信
	fā duǎn-xìn

E-mail

. . . .

E-mail is very widely used, but messaging via certain smartphone apps (**WeChat** in particular) is faster and more frequently used in China. These apps can even be used to pay for taxis, or to buy items in shops.

Business e-mails should be brief and not too familiar or chatty.

What is your e-mail address?	请问你的电子邮箱地址?
	qǐng wèn nǐ de
	diàn-zǐ-yóu-xiāng dì-zhǐ?

How do you spell it?	你如何拼写这个字?
	nǐ rú-hé pīn-xiě zhè gè zì?

All one word	这是一个字
	zhè shì yī-gè zì

My e-mail address is...

我的电子邮箱地址是…
wǒ de diàn-zǐ-yóu-xiāng dì-zhǐ shì...

Can I send an e-mail?

我能发送一封电子邮件吗?
wǒ néng fā-sòng yī-fēng diàn-zǐ-yǒu-jiàn ma?

Internet

• •

Are there any internet cafés here?

这里有网吧吗?
zhè-lǐ yǒu wǎng-bā ma?

How much is it to log on for an hour?

上网一个小时得付多少钱?
shàng-wǎng yī-gè xiǎo-shí děi fù duō-shǎo qián?

Wi-Fi

无线网络
wú-xiàn wǎng-luò

social network

社交网络
shè-jiāo wǎng-luò

app	应用软件 yìng-yòng ruǎn-jiàn
laptop	笔记本电脑 bǐ-jì-běn diàn-nǎo
tablet	平板电脑 píng-bǎn diàn-nǎo
What is the Wi-Fi password?	请问无线网络的密码是多少？ qǐng-wèn wú-xiàn wǎng-luò de mì-mǎ shì duō-shao?
Do you have free Wi-Fi?	请问有免费无线网络吗？ qǐng-wèn yǒu miǎn-fèi wú-xiàn wǎng-luò ma?
Add me on Facebook	请在脸书上加我好友 qǐng zài liǎn-shū shàng jiā wǒ hǎo-yǒu
Is there 3G/4G signal?	有3G/4G的信号吗？ yǒu sān-G/sì-G de xìn-hào ma?

I need to access
my webmail

我需要看我的邮件
wǒ xū-yào kàn wǒ de yóu-jiàn

I would like to
use Skype

我想用Skype即时通信软件
wǒ xiǎng yòng Skype jí-shí
tōng-xìn ruǎn-jiàn

Practicalities

Money

The Renminbi is the currency in China. The units of Renminbi are known as 元 (yuán), 角 (jiǎo) and 分 (fēn). Cash machines are very easy to find on the streets of any city in China, but the only place to exchange money is the bank. If it's a large amount, you need to notify the bank at least one day before. It is fine to use cards in cities now, but street corner shops still don't accept them.

信用卡	xìn-yòng-kǎ	credit card
取钞机	qǔ-chāo-jī	cash machine
收据	shōu-jù	till receipt
美元	měi-yuán	dollars
英镑	yīng-bàng	pounds
汇率	huì-lù	exchange rate

| Where can I change some money? | 我在哪儿能换钱？ |
| | wǒ zài nǎr néng huàn-qián? |

| When does the bank open? | 银行什么时间开门？ |
| | yín-háng shén-me shí-jiān kāi-mén? |

| When does the bank close? | 银行什么时间关门？ |
| | yín-háng shén-me shí-jiān guān-mén? |

| Can I pay with...? | 我可以用 … 付款吗？ |
| | wǒ kě-yǐ yòng … fù-kuǎn ma? |

| Where is the nearest cash machine? | 离这儿最近的取钞机在哪儿？ |
| | lí zhèr zuì-jìn de qǔ-chāo-jī zài-nǎr? |

| Can I use my credit card at the cash machine? | 我能使用信用卡从取钞机取钞吗？ |
| | wǒ néng shǐ-yòng xìn-yòng-kǎ cóng qǔ-chāo-jī qǔ-chāo ma? |

| Do you have any loose change? | 你有零钱吗？ |
| | nǐ yǒu líng-qián ma? |

What is the exchange rate for...?	对 … 的汇率是多少? duì ... de huì-lǜ shì duō-shǎo?

Paying

只收现金 zhǐ shōu xiàn-jīn	cash only
取款　qǔ kuǎn	to withdraw money
储蓄卡　chǔ-xù-kǎ	debit card
借记卡　jiè-jì-kǎ	credit card
非接触式付款 fēi jiē-chù shì fù-kuǎn	contactless payment

How much is it?	多少钱? duō-shǎo qián?

Can I pay by... credit card/ cheque?	我可以使用… 信用卡/支票付款吗? wǒ kě-yǐ shǐ-yòng… xìn-yòng-kǎ/zhī-piào fù-kuǎn ma?

| Is service included? | 服务费已经包括在内了吗？ |
| | fú-wù-fèi yǐ-jīng bāo-kuò zài nèi le ma? |

| Where do I pay? | 我在哪儿付款？ |
| | wǒ zài nǎr fù-kuǎn? |

| I need a receipt please | 请给我一张收据 |
| | qǐng gěi wǒ yī zhāng shōu-jù |

| Do I pay in advance? | 我需要预先付款吗？ |
| | wǒ xū-yào yù-xiān fù-kuǎn ma? |

| Do I need to pay a deposit? | 我需要先付定金吗？ |
| | wǒ xū-yào xiān-fù dìng-jīn ma? |

| I've nothing smaller (no change) | 我没有零钱 |
| | wǒ méi-yǒu líng-qián |

| Can I pay in cash? | 我可以用现金结账吗？ |
| | wǒ kě-yǐ yòng xiàn-jīn jié-zhàng ma? |

Where is the nearest cash machine?	请问最近的取款机在哪儿？ qǐng-wèn zuì-jìn de qǔ-kuǎn-jī zài nǎr?
Is there a credit card charge?	用信用卡要收手续费吗？ yòng xìn-yòng-kǎ yào shōu shǒu-xù-fèi ma?
Is there a discount for senior citizens?	老年人有折扣吗？ lǎo-nián-rén yǒu zhé-kòu ma?
Can you write down the price?	你能把价格写下来吗？ nǐ néng bǎ jià-gé xiě xià-lái ma?

YOU MAY HEAR...

服务费已包括在内，但没包含小费 fú-wù-fèi yǐ bāo-kuò zài nèi, dàn méi bāo-hán xiǎo-fèi	Service is included, but the tip is not
在收银处付款 zài shōu-yín-chù fù-kuǎn	Pay at the till

Luggage

领取行李 lǐng-qǔ xíng-li	baggage reclaim
行李暂存处 xíng-li zàn-cún-chù	left-luggage office
行李推车 xíng-li tuī-chē	luggage trolley

My luggage hasn't arrived	我的行李还没到 wǒ-de xíng-li hái-méi-dào
My suitcase has been damaged on the flight	我的行李箱在飞行中损坏了 wǒ-de xíng-li-xiāng zài fēi-xíng-zhōng sǔn-huài le

Rep:airs

This is broken 这坏了
zhè huài le

Is it worth 值得把它修好吗?
repairing? zhí-de bǎ tā xiū-hǎo ma?

Can you repair...? 你能修理 … 吗?
nǐ néng xiū-lǐ … ma?

this 这件东西
zhè jiàn dōng-xi

these shoes 这些鞋子
zhè xiē xié-zi

my watch 我的手表
wǒ de shǒu-biǎo

Laundry

· · · · · · · · · · · · · · ·

干洗店	gān-xǐ-diàn	dry-cleaner's
洗衣粉	xǐ-yī-fěn	soap powder
去污液	qù-wū-yè	bleach
洗衣机	xǐ-yī-jī	washing machine

| Where can I wash these clothes? | 我在哪儿可以洗这些衣服？ |
| | wǒ zāi nǎr kě-yǐ xǐ zhè-xiē yī-fu? |

| Where is the nearest launderette? | 离这儿最近的干洗店在哪里？ |
| | lí zhèr zuì-jìn-de gān-xǐ-diàn zài-nǎr? |

Complaints

· ·

This does not work/It's broken
这坏了
zhè huài-le

It's dirty
这很脏
zhè hěn-zāng

light
灯
dēng

toilet
厕所
cè-suǒ

heating
暖气
nuǎn-qì

air conditioning
空调
kōng-tiáo

Problems

Can you help me?	你能帮助我吗? nǐ néng bāng-zhù wǒ ma?
I speak very little Mandarin	我只会说一点点普通话 wǒ zhǐ huì shuō yī-diǎn-dian pǔ-tōng-huà
Does anyone here speak English?	这儿有人会说英文吗? zhèr yǒu rén huì shuō yīng-wén ma?
What's the matter?	什么事? shén-me shì?
I would like to speak to whoever is in charge of...	我想和负责人谈谈… wǒ xiǎng hé fù-zé rén tán-tan...
I'm lost	我迷路了 wǒ mí-lù-le

elderly people	老年人 lǎo-nián-rén
disabled people	残疾人 cán-jí-rén
Where can I recycle this?	回收点在哪儿？ huí-shōu-diǎn zài nǎr?
I need to access my online banking	我需要用我的网上银行 wǒ xū-yào yòng wǒ de wǎng-shàng yín-háng
Do you have wheelchairs?	你们有轮椅吗？ nǐ-men yǒu lún-yǐ ma?
Do you have an induction loop?	你们有导听系统吗？ nǐ-men yǒu dǎo-tīng xì-tǒng ma?
I missed my train	我错过了火车 wǒ cuò-guò-le huǒ-chē
plane	飞机 fēi-jī

connection	中转 zhōng-zhuǎn
The coach has left without me	长途客车没等我就开走了 cháng-tú-kè-chē méi děng wǒ jiù kāi-zǒu-le
Can you show me how this works please?	你能向我展示如何使用这件东西吗? nǐ néng xiàng wǒ zhǎn-shì rú-hé shǐ-yòng zhè jiàn dōng-xi ma?
I have lost my money	我丢了钱 wǒ diū le qián
I need to get to...	我需要到达… wǒ xū-yào dào-dá…
Leave me alone!	别打扰我! bié dǎ-rǎo wǒ!
Go away!	走开! zǒu-kāi!

Emergencies

In China, you can ring **120** to call an ambulance,
119 to call the fire brigade and **110** to call the police.

救护车 jiù-hù-chē	ambulance
军警 jūn-jǐng	military police
警察 jǐng-chá	police
消防员 xiāo-fáng-yuán	firemen
消防队 xiāo-fáng-duì	fire brigade
警察局 jǐng-chá-jú	police station
着火 zháo-huǒ	on fire
碰撞 pèng-zhuàng	crash

Help!	救命啊！ jiù-mìng a!
Fire!	着火了！ zháo-huǒ-le!
Can you help me?	你能帮助我吗？ nǐ néng bāng-zhù wǒ ma?

There's been an accident!	出事故了！ chū-shì-gù-le!
Someone has been injured	有人受伤了 yǒu rén shòu-shāng-le
My car crashed	我撞了车 wǒ-zhuàng-le-chē
A thief has stolen my purse	小偷偷了我的钱包 xiǎo-tōu tōu-le wǒ-de qián-bāo
Please call the police	请叫警察 qǐng-jiào jǐng-chá
Please call an ambulance	请叫救护车 qǐng-jiào jiù-hù-chē
Where is the police station?	警察局在哪儿？ jǐng-chá-jú zài nǎr?
I've been... robbed/attacked	我被 … 抢了/殴打了 wǒ-bèi … qiǎng-le/ōu-dǎ-le

Someone's stolen... my bag/my money	某人偷了 … 我的包/我的钱 mǒu rén tōu-le … wǒ de bāo/ wǒ de qián
My car has been stolen	我的车被盗了 wǒ de chē bèi dào-le
I've been raped	我被人强奸了 wǒ bèi rén qiáng-jiān-le
I want to speak to a policewoman	我想和一名女警员谈话 wǒ xiǎng hé yī-míng nǚ-jǐng-yuán tán-huà
I need to make a telephone call	我需要打个电话 wǒ xū-yào dǎ gè diàn-huà
I need a report for my insurance	我需要一份报告给保险公司 wǒ xū-yào yī-fèn bào-gào gěi bǎo-xiǎn-gōng-sī
How much is the fine?	罚多少钱? fá duō-shǎo qián?

Health

Pharmacy

Pharmacies normally have a large green cross sign either at the door, or hanging from the wall. Finding a pharmacy in any city is easy. Most are open all week, and some are 24/7.

药店　yào-diàn	pharmacy/chemist
值班药剂师 zhí-bān yào-jì-shī	duty chemist

As a tourist, you are not advised to drink tap water in China. Furthermore, due to the spices used in food (that you may not be used to), having medicine for diarrhoea is important. Watch out for mosquitoes too, they are very common.

Can you give me something for...?	你能给我 … 的药吗?
	nǐ néng gěi wǒ … de yào ma?

a headache	头疼
	tóu-téng

car sickness	晕车
	yūn-chē

a cough	咳嗽
	ké-sou

diarrhoea	拉肚子
	lā-dù-zi

Is it safe for children?	孩子吃这种药安全吗?
	hái-zi chī zhè-zhǒng yào ān-quán ma?

How much should I give him?	我应该给他服用多少剂量?
	wǒ yīng-gāi gěi tā fú-yòng duō-shǎo jì-liàng?

每日三次··· měi-rì sān-cì...	Three times a day...
吃饭前/吃饭时/ 吃饭后 chī-fàn qián/chī-fàn shí/chī-fàn hòu	before/with/after meals

asthma	哮喘	xiào-chuǎn
condom	避孕套	bì-yùn-tào
contact lenses	隐形眼镜	yǐn-xíng yǎn-jìng
inhaler	吸入器	xī-rù qì
morning-after pill	事后避孕药	shì-hòu bì-yùn yào
mosquito bite	蚊虫叮咬	wén-chóng dīng-yǎo
mosquito repellent	驱蚊水	qū-wén-shuǐ
painkillers	止痛药	zhǐ-tòng-yào
period	月经	yuè-jīng
the Pill	避孕药	bì-yùn yào

Health

sanitary towel 卫生巾	wèi-shēng-jīn
tampon 棉条	mián-tiáo

Doctor

. . . .

呼吸困难 hū-xī-kùn-nán	breathing difficulties
心脏病 xīn-zàng-bìng	heart disease
心跳 xīn-tìao	heartbeat
高/低血压 gāo/dī-xuè-yā	high/low blood pressure
糖尿病 táng-niào-bìng	diabetes
贫血症 pín-xuè-zhèng	anaemia
医院 yī-yuàn	hospital
急诊室 jí-zhěn-shì	A&E
当地健康中心 dāng-dì jiàn-kāng-zhōng-xīn	local health centre

我生病了
wǒ shēng-bìng-le
I feel ill

你发烧吗?
nǐ fā-shāo ma?
Do you have a temperature?

不，我 … 疼
bù, wǒ … téng
No, I have a pain in my...

Health

I need a doctor	我需要看医生 wǒ xū-yào kàn yī-shēng
I'm diabetic	我患有糖尿病 wǒ huàn-yǒu táng-niào-bìng
I'm pregnant	我怀孕了 wǒ huái-yùn-le
I'm on the pill	我一直在吃避孕药 wǒ yī-zhí zài chī bì-yùn-yào
I'm allergic to penicillin	我对青霉素过敏 wǒ duì qīng-méi-sù guò-mǐn

I'm having breathing difficulties at the moment	我现在呼吸困难 wǒ xiàn-zài hū-xī-kùn-nán
I have been suffering from heart disease for a long time	我长期患有心脏病 wǒ cháng-qī huàn-yǒu xīn-zàng-bìng
My heart is beating very fast at the moment	我现在的心跳很快 wǒ xiàn-zài-de xīn-tiào hěn kuài
I have been suffering from high blood pressure for years	我多年来一直患有高血压 wǒ duō nián lái yī-zhí huàn-yǒu gāo xuè-yā
I have been suffering from low blood pressure for years	我多年来一直患有低血压 wǒ duō nián lái yī-zhí huàn-yǒu dī xuè-yā

I am anaemic	我患有贫血症 wǒ hùan-yǒu pín-xuè-zhèng
Will I have to pay?	我必须付钱吗? wǒ bì-xū fù-qián ma?
cystitis	尿路感染 niào-lù gǎn-rǎn
drug abuse	吸毒 xī-dú
epilepsy	癫痫 diān-xián
food poisoning	食物中毒 shí-wù zhòng-dú
headache	头疼 tóu-téng
sprain	扭伤 niǔ-shāng

STI/STD (sexually transmitted infection/disease)	性病 xìng-bìng
GP (general practitioner)	家庭医生 jiā-tíng yī-shēng
A&E (accident and emergency)	急诊科 jí-zhěn-kē
I'm allergic to...	我对 … 过敏 wǒ duì … guò-mǐn
animal hair	动物毛发 dòng-wù máo-fà
pollen	花粉 huā-fěn
dairy	乳制品 rǔ-zhì-pǐn
gluten	谷蛋白 gǔ-dàn-bái

nuts	坚果 jiān-guǒ
I have a prescription for...	医生给我开了 … 药 yī-shēng gěi wǒ kāi le … yào
I've run out of medication	我的药吃完了 wǒ de yào chī wán le
I have a... intolerance	我有 … 不耐受症 wǒ yǒu … bù nài-shòu zhèng
How much will it cost?	得要多少钱? děi yào duō-shǎo qián?
Can you give me a receipt for the insurance?	你能给我一张保险公司要的收据吗? nǐ néng gěi wǒ yī-zhāng bǎo-xiǎn-gōng-sī yào-de shōu-jù ma?

你必须去医院 nǐ bì-xū qù yī-yuàn	You will have to go into hospital
不严重 bù yán-zhòng	It's not serious
请勿饮酒 qǐng-wù yǐn-jiǔ	Do not drink alcohol
你喝酒吗？ nǐ hē-jiǔ ma?	Do you drink?
你抽烟吗？ nǐ chōu-yān ma?	Do you smoke?
你吸毒吗？ nǐ xī-dú ma?	Do you take drugs?

Health

arm	胳膊	gē-bo
back	背	bèi
chest	胸	xiōng
ear	耳朵	ěr-duo
eye	眼睛	yǎn-jīng
foot	脚	jiǎo
head	头	tóu
heart	心脏	xīn-zàng

leg	腿	tuǐ
neck	脖子	bó-zi
toe	脚趾	jiǎo-zhǐ
tooth	牙齿	yá-chǐ
wrist	手腕	shǒu-wàn

Dentist

• •

I need a dentist	我需要看牙医 wǒ xū-yào kàn yá-yī
He/She has toothache	他/她牙疼 tā/tā yá-téng
Can you do a temporary filling?	你能作临时的补牙吗? nǐ néng zuò lín-shí de bǔ-yá ma?
It hurts	疼 téng

Can you give me something for the pain?	你能给我一些止疼药吗? nǐ néng gěi wǒ yī-xiē zhǐ-téng-yào ma?
Can you repair my dentures?	你能补我的假牙吗? nǐ néng bǔ wǒ-de jiǎ-yá ma?
How much will it be?	得要多少钱? děi yào duō-shǎo qián?

YOU MAY HEAR...

我必须把它取出来 wǒ bì-xū bǎ tā qǔ chū lái	I'll have to take it out
你需要补一颗牙 nǐ xū-yào bǔ yī kē yá	You need a filling
可能会有一些疼痛 kě néng huì yǒu yī xiē téng-tòng	This might hurt a little

Eating out

Eating places

| 咖啡厅 kā-fēi-tīng | café |
| 酒吧 jiǔ-bā | bar |

In China, bars stay open very late, until the early hours of the morning. You'll often find bands or singers performing in bars. The idea of a café in China is slightly different from what you may be used to. They are quite expensive, serve big meals, and are lavishly decorated.

What would you like to drink?	你想喝什么? nǐ xiǎng hē shén-me?
tea, please	茶, 谢谢 chá, xiè-xie
a coffee	一杯咖啡 yī-bēi kā-fēi

a beer	一支啤酒
	yī-zhī pí-jiǔ
an orange juice	一杯橙汁
	yī-bēi chéng-zhī
with lemon	加柠檬
	jiā níng-méng
no sugar	不加糖
	bù-jiā táng
for two	要两份
	yào liǎng fèn
for me	给我
	gěi wǒ
for him/her	给他/她
	gěi tā/tā
with ice	加冰
	jiā-bīng
a bottle of	一瓶矿泉水
mineral water	yī-píng kuàng-quán-shuǐ

| sparkling | 有汽泡的 |
| | yǒu qì-pào-de |

| still | 无汽泡的 |
| | wú qì-pào-de |

At a tea house

People often go to tea houses to play **mahjong** (a traditional game involving tiles) or card games with their friends. These tea houses also serve food. In Guangdong province and Hong Kong, you can get delicious **dim-sum** in tea houses.

中国茶 zhōng-guó-chá	Chinese tea
红/绿茶 hóng/lǜ-chá	red/green tea
一壶茶 yī-hú-chá	a pot of tea
开水 kāi-shuǐ	boiled water
苦 kǔ	bitter
小费 xiǎo-fèi	tip (for service)
茶楼/茶馆 chá-lóu/chá-guǎn	tea house

I would like to drink Chinese red/green tea	我想喝中国红/绿茶 wǒ xiǎng hē zhōng-guó-hóng/ lǜ-chá
How much is a pot of tea?	请问一壶茶多少钱? qǐng wèn yī-hú-chá duō-shǎo qián?
Please add more boiled water	请加开水 qǐng jiā kāi-shuǐ
This kind of tea is too bitter	这种茶太苦了 zhè zhǒng chá tài-kǔ-le

YOU MAY HEAR...

| 你想喝哪种中国茶?
nǐ xiǎng hē nǎ-zhǒng zhōng-guó-chá? | What kind of Chinese tea would you like to drink? |

In a restaurant

FACE TO FACE

我想预定一张 … 人的桌子
wǒ xiǎng yù-dìng yī zhāng … rén-de zhuō-zi
I'd like to book a table for ... people

好，什么时间的?
hǎo, shén-me shí-jiān-de?
Yes, when for?

今晚…/明晚…/八点
jīn-wǎn…/míng-wǎn…/bā-diǎn
Tonight.../for tomorrow night.../at 8 o'clock

The menu please	请拿菜单给我 qǐng ná cài-dān gěi wǒ
What is the dish of the day?	今天有什么招牌菜? jīn-tiān yǒu shén-me zhāo-pái-cài?
Do you have a tourist menu?	你们有为游客准备的菜单吗? nǐ-men yǒu wèi yóu-kè zhǔn-bèi-de cài-dān ma?

What is the speciality of the house?	这里的招牌菜是什么？ zhè-lǐ-de zhāo-pái-cài shì shén-me?
Can you tell me what this is?	请告诉我这是什么菜？ qǐng gào-sù wǒ zhè shì shén-me cài?
I'll have this	我要点这道菜 wǒ yào diǎn zhè-dào cài
Could we have a bottle of mineral water please?	请再给我们拿一支矿泉水好吗？ qǐng zài gěi wǒ-men ná yī zhī kuàng-quán-shuǐ hǎo-ma?
The bill please	我要埋单 wǒ yào mái-dān
homemade	自制的 zì-zhì de
local delicacy	当地特色美食 dāng-dì tè-sè měi-shí
Is there a set menu?	有套餐吗？ yǒu tào-cān ma?

We would like a table for ... people please	我们 … 位	wǒ-men … wèi
This isn't what I ordered	我点的不是这个	wǒ diǎn de bù-shì zhè-ge
The ... is too...	这个 … 太 … 了	zhè-ge … tài … le

cold	冷的	lěng de
greasy	油腻的	yóu-nì de
rare	生的	shēng de
salty	咸的	xián de
spicy	辣的	là de
warm	热的	rè de
well-cooked	熟的	shú de

Dietary requirements

Vegetarianism is gradually being accepted in China. Although most restaurants don't have vegetarian dishes as such, there will be many vegetable-based dishes to choose from. It is worth checking that these do not contain minced meat, as this is often added to enhance the flavour of a dish.

Are there any vegetarian restaurants here?	这里有斋菜饭馆吗? zhè-lǐ yǒu zhāi-cài fàn-guǎn ma?
Do you have any vegetarian dishes?	你们这里有斋菜吗? nǐ-men zhè-lǐ yǒu zhāi-cài ma?
Which dishes have no meat?	哪些菜里没有肉? nǎ-xiē cài lǐ méi-yǒu ròu?
Which dishes have no fish?	哪些菜里没有鱼? nǎ-xiē cài lǐ méi-yǒu yú?
What fish dishes do you have?	你们有哪些鱼? nǐ-men yǒu nǎ-xiē yú?
What do you recommend?	你能建议我点些什么菜吗? nǐ néng jiàn-yì wǒ diǎn-xiē shén-me cài ma?

As there are more and more Buddhists in the country, you may be able to find strict vegetarian restaurants, especially in big cities. Some of these places do vegetarian versions of popular meat dishes. This food is made to look and feel like meat, but is completely meat-free.

coeliac disease	腹腔疾病	fù-qiāng jí-bìng
dairy	乳制品	rǔ-zhì-pǐn
gluten	谷蛋白	gǔ-dàn-bái
halal	清真	qīng-zhēn
organic	有机的	yǒu-jī de
nuts	坚果	jiān-guǒ
vegan	纯素食者	chún sù-shí-zhě
wheat	谷物	gǔ-wù

I have a... allergy	我对 … 过敏	wǒ duì … guò-mǐn
Is it... -free?	这里面有 … 吗？	zhè lǐ-miàn yǒu … ma?
I don't eat...	我不吃…	wǒ bù chī...

138

Spirits and liqueurs

What liqueurs do you have?	你们有哪些烈酒? nǐ-men yǒu nǎ-xiē liè-jiǔ?	

白兰地	bái-lán-dì	brandy
威士忌	wēi-shì-jì	whisky
茅台酒	máo-tái-jiǔ	maotai, a famous Chinese grain spirit which is quite strong
二锅头	èr-guō-tóu	erguotou, a well-known and cheap sorghum spirit which is quite strong
女儿红	nǔ-ér-hóng	Chinese rice wines

Menu reader

Soft drinks

七喜 qī-xǐ
Lemonade

鲜榨橙汁 xiān-zhà-chéng-zhī
Freshly squeezed orange juice

中国绿茶 zhōng-guó-lǜ-chá
Chinese green tea

Beers

青岛啤酒 qīng-dǎo pí-jiǔ
Qingdao beer

燕京啤酒 yān-jīng pí-jiǔ
Yanjing beer

珠江啤酒 zhū-jiāng pí-jiǔ
Zhujiang beer

Wines

长城牌白葡萄酒 cháng-chéng-pái bái
pú-táo-jiǔ
Changcheng white wine

长城牌红葡萄酒 cháng-chéng-pái hóng
pú-táo-jiǔ
Changcheng red wine

Spirits and liqueurs

二锅头 èr-guō-tóu
Erguotou sorghum spirit

茅台酒 máo-tái-jiǔ
Maotai grain spirit

女儿红 nǚ-ér-hóng
Nüerhong rice wine

Soups

豆腐杂菜汤 dòu-fu zá cài tāng
Tofu and mixed vegetable soup

鸡蛋西红柿汤 jī-dàn xī-hóng-shì tāng
Egg and tomato soup

鸡粒玉米羹 jī-lì yù-mǐ gēng
Diced chicken and sweetcorn soup

鸡肉蘑菇汤 jī-ròu mó-gu tāng
Chicken and mushroom soup

酸辣汤 suān-là-tāng
Hot and sour soup

鱼片豆腐汤 yú-piàn dòu-fu-tāng
Shredded fish and tofu/bean curd soup

Seafood

豉汁蒸鳝鱼 chǐ-zhī zhēng shàn-yú
Steamed eel with black bean sauce

豉汁蒸鲜鱿 chǐ-zhī zhēng xiān-yóu
Steamed squid with black bean sauce

带子炒芦笋 dài-zǐ chǎo lú-sǔn
Stir-fried scallops with asparagus

炖鲍鱼 dùn bào-yú
Braised abalone

海鲜粉丝煲 hǎi-xiān fěn-sī bāo
Hot-pot of mixed seafood with vermicelli

红烧鲤鱼 hóng-shāo lǐ-yú
Stewed carp with soya sauce, ginger and
Chinese wine

姜葱炒龙虾 jiāng cōng chǎo lóng-xiā
Stir-fried lobster with ginger and spring onions

姜葱蒸带子 jiāng cōng zhēng dāi-zi
Steamed scallops with ginger and spring onions

姜葱清蒸鲢鱼 jiāng cōng qīng-zhēng lián-yú
Steamed chub with ginger and spring onion

姜葱蒸鲈鱼 jiāng cōng zhēng lú-yú
Steamed sea bass with ginger and spring onions

姜葱清蒸三文鱼 jiāng cōng qīng-zhēng
sān-wén-yú
Steamed salmon with ginger and spring onion

女儿红酒蒸螃蟹 nǔ-ér-hóng jiǔ zhēng
páng-xiè
Steamed crab with Chinese rice wine

清炒大虾 qīng-chǎo dà-xiā
Stir-fried tiger prawns

清炒鲜鱿 qīng-chǎo xiān-yóu
Stir-fried squid

西红柿小鲍鱼煲 xī-hóng-shì xiǎo
bào-yú bāo
Hot-pot of stewed abalone with tomato

Poultry

白切鸡 bái-qiē-jī
Boiled chicken

红烧鸡 hóng-shāo-jī
Stewed diced chicken with soya sauce and ginger

鸡块炒蘑菇 jī kuài chǎo mó-gu
Stir-fried diced chicken with mushrooms

鸡片炒芦笋 jī-piàn chǎo lú-sǔn
Stir-fried shredded chicken with asparagus

姜葱炒鸡块 jiāng cōng chǎo jī kuài
Stir-fried diced chicken with ginger and spring
onions

烤鸡 kǎo-jī
Roast chicken

辣子鸡丁 là-zi jī-dīng
Stir-fried diced chicken with chilli

栗子炖鸡 lì-zi dùn jī
Braised chicken with chestnuts

腰果炒鸡丁 yāo-guǒ chǎo jī-dīng
Stir-fried diced chicken with cashew nuts

Beef

豉汁辣椒炒牛肉 chǐ-zhī là-jiāo chǎo niú-ròu
Stir-fried beef with black bean sauce and chilli

红烧牛肉 hóng-shāo niú-ròu
Stewed beef with soya sauce and ginger

姜葱炒牛肉 jiāng cōng chǎo niú-ròu
Stir-fried beef with ginger and spring onions

辣子牛肉煲 là-zi niú-ròu bāo
Hot-pot diced beef with chilli

牛肉炒菠萝 niú-ròu chǎo bō-lúo
Stir-fried beef with pineapple

土豆炖牛肉 tǔ-dòu dùn niú-ròu
Braised beef with potatoes

Duck, pork and lamb

叉烧（烤猪肉） chā-shāo (kǎo-zhū-ròu)
Roast pork

豉汁蒸排骨 chǐ-zhī zhēng pái-gǔ
Steamed pork spare ribs with black bean sauce

串烧羊肉块 chuàn-shāo yáng-ròu-kuài
Diced lamb kebab

炖羊肉 dùn yáng-ròu
Braised diced lamb with soya sauce and ginger

咕噜肉 gū-lū ròu
Sweet and sour pork

红烧肉 hóng-shāo ròu
Stewed pork

椒盐排骨 jiāo-yán pái-gǔ
Roast pork spare ribs with pepper powder and salt

烤鸭 kǎo yā
Roast duck

辣椒炒鸭片 là-jiāo chǎo yā-piàn
Stir-fried shredded duck with chilli

辣羊肉丝炒胡萝卜片 là yáng-ròu-sī chǎo hú-luó-bo-piàn
Stir-fried shredded lamb with sliced carrots and chilli

辣子炒羊肉 là-zi chǎo yáng-ròu
Stir-fried chicken and lamb with chilli and ginger

辣子肉丁 là-zi ròu-dīng
Stir-fried diced pork with chilli

肉片炒黄瓜 ròu-piàn chǎo-huáng-guā
Stir-fried shredded pork with cucumber

肉片炒芦笋 ròu-piàn chǎo lú-sǔn
Stir-fried shredded pork with asparagus

肉丝炒青椒 ròu-sī chǎo qīng-jiāo
Stir-fried shredded pork with green peppers

酸梅汁蒸鸭块 suān-méi-zhī zhēng yā-kuài
Stewed diced duck with prune sauce

酸甜排骨 suān-tián pái-gǔ
Sweet and sour pork spare ribs

香酥鸭 xiāng-sū yā
Crispy duck

羊肉煲 yáng-ròu bāo
Lamb hot-pot

鱼香肉片 yú-xiāng ròu-piàn
Stir-fried shredded pork with mushroom and chilli

Vegetables and tofu/bean curd

海鲜豆腐煲 hǎi-xiān dòu-fu bāo
Hot-pot of tofu/bean curd and mixed seafood

蚝油炒菜心 háo-yóu chǎo cài-xīn
Stir-fried Chinese green vegetables with oyster sauce

蚝油炒芦笋 háo-yóu chǎo lú-sǔn
Stir-fried asparagus with oyster sauce

红烧素豆腐 hóng-shāo sù dòu-fu
Braised tofu (without meat)

凉拌海带丝 liáng-bàn-hǎi-dài-sī
Sliced seaweed marinated with soya sauce, garlic,
vinegar and sesame oil

凉拌黄瓜丝 liáng-bàn huáng-guā-sī
Sliced cucumber marinated with soya sauce, garlic,
vinegar and sesame oil

肉末酿豆腐 ròu-mò niàng dòu-fu
Minced pork stuffed with tofu/bean curd

素炒豆芽 sù-chǎo dòu-yá
Stir-fried bean sprouts

蒜蓉炒大白菜 suàn-róng chǎo dà-bái-cài
Stir-fried Chinese leaf with garlic

蒜蓉炒蘑菇 suàn-róng chǎo mó-gu
Stir-fried mushrooms with garlic

蒜蓉炒青椒 suàn-róng chǎo qīng-jiāo
Stir-fried green peppers with garlic

蒜蓉蚝油炒青菜 suàn-róng háo-yóu chǎo
qīng-cài
Stir-fried Chinese greens with garlic and oyster sauce

虾仁酿豆腐 xiā-rén niàng dòu-fu
Prawns stuffed with tofu/bean curd

鱼香茄子 yú-xiāng qié-zi
Hot aubergine

Rice, noodles and dumplings

白米饭 bái mǐ-fàn
Steamed rice

蛋炒饭 dàn chǎo fàn
Egg fried rice

海鲜炒面 hǎi-xiān chǎo miàn
Fried noodles with seafood

海鲜汤面 hǎi-xiān tāng-miàn
Noodle soup with mixed seafood

龙虾炒面 lóng-xiā chǎo-miàn
Stir-fried lobster with noodles

什菜素汤面 shí-cài sù tāng miàn
Noodle soup with mixed vegetables

素菜饺子 sù-cài jiǎo-zi
Vegetable dumplings

素炒面 sù chǎo miàn
Fried noodles

鲜虾韭菜饺子 xiān-xiā jiǔ-cài jiǎo-zi
Prawn and chive dumplings

羊肉饺子 yáng-ròu jiǎo-zi
Minced lamb dumplings

蒸馒头 zhēng mán-tou
Steamed bun

猪肉大白菜饺子 zhū-ròu dà-bái-cài jiǎo-zi
Pork and Chinese leaf dumplings

Eggs

鸡蛋炒西红柿 jī-dàn chǎo xī-hóng-shì
Stir-fried eggs with tomato

鸡蛋炒虾仁 jī-dàn chǎo xiā-rén
Stir-fried eggs with peeled prawns

For vegetarians

干煸四季豆 gān-biān sì-jì-dòu
Dry-fried green beans

蒜蓉空心菜 suàn-róng kōng-xīn-cài
Stir-fried water spinach with garlic

蒜蓉西兰花 suàn-róng xī-lán-huā
Stir-fried broccoli with garlic

白灼菜心 bái-zhuó cài-xīn
Stir-fired choy sum in soy sauce

麻婆豆腐 má-pó dòu-fu
Mapo tofu in chilli bean paste sauce

扁豆面 biǎn-dòu miàn
Noodles in lentil soup

Reference

Measurements and quantities
• • • • • • • • • • • • • • • • • • • •

Liquids 液体

1/2 litre of...
半升…
bàn-shēng...

a litre of...
一升…
yī-shēng...

1/2 bottle of...
半瓶…
bàn-píng...

a bottle of...
一瓶…
yī-píng...

a glass of...
一杯…
yī-bēi...

Weights 重量

1 斤 (jīn) = 0.5 kilo

100 grams	100克 yī-bǎi kè
1/2 kilo of...	半公斤··· bàn gōng-jīn...
a kilo of...	一公斤··· yī gōng-jīn...

Food 食品

a slice of...	一片··· yī-piàn...
a portion of...	一份··· yī-fèn...
a dozen...	十二个··· shí-èr gè...
a box of...	一盒··· yī-hé...
a packet of...	一包··· yī-bāo...

a tin of...	一罐··· yī-guàn...
a can of...(beer)	一罐···（啤酒） yī-guàn... (pí-jiǔ)

Miscellaneous 其它杂物

...yuan-worth of...	···元的··· ...yuán-de...
a quarter	四分之一 sì-fēn-zhī-yī
20 per cent	百分之二十 bǎi-fēn-zhī-èr-shí
more than...	多于··· duō-yú...
less than...	少于··· shǎo-yú...
double	两倍 liǎng-bèi

Numbers

. . . .

0	零	líng
1	一	yī
2	二	èr
3	三	sān
4	四	sì
5	五	wǔ
6	六	liù
7	七	qī
8	八	bā
9	九	jiǔ
10	十	shí
11	十一	shí-yī
12	十二	shí-èr
13	十三	shí-sān
14	十四	shí-sì
15	十五	shí-wǔ
16	十六	shí-liù
17	十七	shí-qī

18	十八	shí-bā
19	十九	shí-jiǔ
20	二十	èr-shí
21	二十一	èr-shí-yī
22	二十二	èr-shí-èr
23	二十三	èr-shí-sān
24	二十四	èr-shí-sì
25	二十五	èr-shí-wǔ
26	二十六	èr-shí-liù
27	二十七	èr-shí-qī
28	二十八	èr-shí-bā
29	二十九	èr-shí-jiǔ
30	三十	sān-shí
40	四十	sì-shí
50	五十	wǔ-shí
60	六十	liù-shí
70	七十	qī-shí
80	八十	bā-shí
90	九十	jiǔ-shí
100	一百	yī-bǎi
110	一百一十	yī-bǎi-yī-shí

1000	一千	yī-qiān
2000	两千	liǎng-qiān
million	一百万	yī-bǎi-wàn
billion	十亿	shí-yì
10 million	一千万	yī-qiān-wàn
100 million	一亿	yī yì

1st	第一 dì-yī		2nd	第二 dì-èr	
3rd	第三 dì-sān		4th	第四 dì-sì	
5th	第五 dì-wǔ		6th	第六 dì-liù	
7th	第七 dì-qī		8th	第八 dì-bā	
9th	第九 dì-jiǔ		10th	第十 dì-shí	

15th	第十五	dì-shí-wǔ
20th	第二十	dì-èr-shí
50th	第五十	dì-wǔ-shí
100th	第一百	dì-yī-bǎi
101st	第一百零一	dì-yī-bǎi-líng-yī
110th	第一百一十	dì-yī-bǎi-yī-shí
1,000th	第一千	dì-yī-qián

Fractions and percentages

½	二分之一	èr fēn zhī yī
⅓	三分之一	sān fēn zhī yī
¼	四分之一	sì fēn zhī yī
⅔	三分之二	sān fēn zhī èr
0.5	零点五	líng diǎn wǔ
3.5	三点五	sān diǎn wǔ
6.89	六点八九	liù diǎn bā jiǔ
10%	百分之十	bǎi fēn zhī shí
100%	百分之百	bǎi fēn zhī bǎi

Days and months

Days 日

Monday	星期一	xīng-qī-yī
Tuesday	星期二	xīng-qīng-èr
Wednesday	星期三	xīng-qīng-sān
Thursday	星期四	xīng-qīng-sì
Friday	星期五	xīng-qīng-wǔ
Saturday	星期六	xīng-qīng-liù
Sunday	星期日	xīng-qīng-rì

Seasons 季节

spring	春天	chūn-tiān
summer	夏天	xià-tiān
autumn	秋天	qiū-tiān
winter	冬天	dōng-tiān

Months 月

January	一月	yī-yuè
February	二月	èr-yuè
March	三月	sān-yuè
April	四月	sì-yuè
May	五月	wǔ-yuè
June	六月	liù-yuè
July	七月	qī-yuè
August	八月	bā-yuè
September	九月	jiǔ-yuè
October	十月	shí-yuè
November	十一月	shí-yī-yuè
December	十二月	shí-èr-yuè

What is today's date?
今天是几月几日？
jīn-tiān shì jǐ yuè jǐ rì?

What day is it today?
今天是星期几？
jīn-tiān shì xīng-qī jǐ?

5th March 2017
今天是2017年3月5日
jīn-tiān shì èr-líng-yī-qī-nián sān-yuè-wǔ-rì

on the 20th	在20日	zài èr-shí-rì
the first of January	1月1日	yī-yuè-yī-rì
in 2017	在2017年	zài èr-líng-yī-liù-nián
in the nineteenth century	在十九世纪	zài shí-jiǔ-shì-jì
in the nineties	在九十年代	zài jiǔ-shí nián-dài
on Saturday	在星期六	zài xīng-qī-liù
every Saturday	每逢星期六	měi-féng xīng-qī-liù
this Saturday	本星期六	běn xīng-qī-liù
next Saturday	下星期六	xià xīng-qī-liù

last Saturday	上星期六
	shàng xīng-qī-liù
in June	在六月份
	zài liù-yuè-fèn
at the beginning of June	在六月初
	zài liù-yuè chū
at the end of June	在六月末
	zài liù-yuè mò
before summer	夏天之前
	xià-tiān zhī-qián
during the summer	夏季
	xià-jì
after summer	夏天之后
	xià-tiān zhī-hòu

Time

What time is it please?	请问现在几点了? qǐng wèn xiàn-zài jǐ-diǎn-le?
It's...	现在是… xiàn-zài-shì...
2 o'clock	两点钟 liǎng-diǎn-zhōng
3 o'clock	三点钟 sān-diǎn-zhōng
6 o'clock	六点钟 liù-diǎn-zhōng
1 o'clock	一点钟 yī-diǎn-zhōng
It's midday	现在是中午十二点钟 xiàn-zài shì zhōng-wǔ shí-èr-diǎn-zhōng

It's midnight	现在是半夜十二点钟 xiàn-zài shì bàn-yè shí-èr-diǎn-zhōng
9	九点 jiǔ-diǎn
9.10	九点十分 jiǔ-diǎn-shí-fēn
quarter past 9	九点一刻 jiǔ-diǎn-yī-kè
9.20	九点二十分 jiǔ-diǎn-èr-shí-fēn
half past 9	九点半 jiǔ-diǎn-bàn
9.35	九点三十五分 jiǔ-diǎn-sān-shí-wǔ-fēn
quarter to 10	差一刻十点 chà-yī-kè-shí-diǎn
5 to 10	差五分十点 chà-wǔ-fēn-shí-diǎn

Time phrases

When does it...?	什么时间…? shén-me shí-jiān…?
open	开门 kāi-mén
close	关门 guān-mén
begin	开始 kāi-shǐ
finish	结束 jié-shù
at 3 o'clock	三点 sān-diǎn
before 3 o'clock	三点之前 sān-diǎn zhī-qián
after 3 o'clock	三点之后 sān-diǎn zhī-hòu

today	今天 jīn-tiān
tonight	今晚 jīn-wǎn
tomorrow	明天 míng-tiān
yesterday	昨天 zuó-tiān

前天 qián-tiān	the day before yesterday
后天 hòu-tiān	the day after tomorrow
昨天上午/下午/晚上 zuó-tiān shàng-wǔ/ xià-wǔ/wǎn-shàng	yesterday morning/ afternoon/evening
明天上午/下午/晚上 míng-tiān shàng-wǔ/ xià-wǔ/wǎn-shàng	tomorrow morning/ afternoon/evening
第二天 dì-èr-tiān	the next day

Public holidays

- -

1 January	**New Year's Day** (yuán-dàn)
4/5/6 April	**Tomb Sweeping Day** (qīng-míng-jié)
1 May	**Labour Day** (wǔ-yī-láo-dòng-jié)
15 August (lunar calendar)	**Mid-Autumn Day** (zhōng-qiū-jié)
1 October	**National Day** (guó-qìng-jié)

Chinese New Year (chūn-jié) is the biggest and longest public holiday in China. It falls on a different day each year in the western solar calendar (normally the first day of the Chinese New Year ranges from the end of January to the middle of February). It always starts on the first day of each year of the Chinese lunar calendar. The celebration lasts for fifteen days.

Traditionally, families gather together, children receive money in 'red envelopes' and everyone helps make and eat a feast of jiǎo-zi 饺子 (steamed dumplings with a thin skin, usually filled with pork and vegetables). Throughout this festival it is traditional to wish people wealth and happiness by saying gōng-xǐ fā-cái 恭喜发财.

Yuán-xiāo-jié 元宵节 **Yuanxiao Festival**, or **Lantern Festival**, is celebrated on the 15th day of Chinese New Year. The traditional food eaten at this festival is called yuán-xiāo, or tāng-yuán 汤圆, a traditional sweet dumpling made of glutinous rice, with various fillings.

Duān-wǔ-jié 端午节, the **Dragon Boat Festival**, is celebrated on the 5th day of the 5th month of the Chinese lunar calendar. The two main activities which take place at this time are dragon boat racing and eating zòng-zi 粽子 (dates or meat covered in sticky rice and wrapped in bamboo leaves). Both of these activities originate from the festival's traditional associations with the poet and statesman Qu Yuan. According to legend, he committed suicide by jumping into the Miluo River after his loyalty to the emperor was not rewarded. The story goes that local people took to their boats and threw zongzi into the river to feed the fish, in the hope of rescuing his body.

Guó-qìng-jié 国庆节 **National Day**, on 1 October, commemorates the anniversary of the founding of the People's Republic of China (1949). The PRC was declared by Chairman Mao Zedong, in Tiananmen Square in Beijing.

Zhōng-qiū-jié 中秋节 **Mid-Autumn Festival**, or **Moon-Gazing Festival**, is celebrated on the 15th day of the 8th month of the Chinese lunar calendar. Traditionally families gather to observe the moon and eat yuè-bǐng 月饼, mooncakes (round cakes made with a variety of sweet fillings including bean paste, egg and peanut). The roundness of both the full moon and the cakes symbolise the unity of the family.

Qīng-míng 清明节, sometimes translated literally as the **Clear and Bright Festival**, or the **Tomb Sweeping Festival**, is celebrated on the 4th, 5th or 6th of April. It is traditionally the time when Chinese families visit graves to honour their dead ancestors. At this time people also avoid eating hot food (the festival is sometimes also referred to as hán-shí-jié 寒食节 or **Cold Food Festival**).

The good news for visitors going to China is that most of the shops and restaurants, and almost all hotels, parks and museums, remain open during the national holidays. The buses, trains and planes operate during national holidays as well.

Signs and notices

• •

When you are in China, you will see some written Chinese characters in airports, hotels, restaurants, parks and stations. You will need to know what they mean in English.

General

入口	rù-kǒu	entrance
出口	chū-kǒu	exit
小心	xiǎo-xīn	caution
女厕	nǚ-cè	women's toilet
男厕	nán-cè	men's toilet
火警警报器	huǒ-jǐng jǐng-bào-qì	fire alarm
灭火器	miè-huǒ-qì	fire extinguisher
上	shàng	up
下	xià	down
左	zuǒ	left
右	yòu	right
止步	zhǐ-bù	keep out

失物招领	shī-wù-zhāo-lǐng	lost property
拉	lā	pull
推	tuī	push
有人	yǒu-rén	occupied
危险	wēi-xiǎn	danger
饮用水	yǐn-yòng-shuǐ	drinking water
非饮用水	fēi-yǐn-yòng-shuǐ	non-drinking water
禁止入内	jìn-zhǐ-rù-nèi	no entry
禁止吸烟	jìn-zhǐ-xī-yān	no smoking
禁止游泳	jìn-zhǐ-yóu-yǒng	no swimming
警报器	jǐng-bào-qì	alarm

Airport/station

机场	jī-chǎng	airport
电梯	diàn-tī	lift/elevator
地铁站	dì-tiě-zhàn	metro station
火车站	huǒ-chē-zhàn	railway station

公共汽车站	gōng-gòng-qì-chē-zhàn	bus station
行李认领	xíng-li-rèn-lǐng	baggage reclaim
免税店	miǎn-shuì-diàn	duty-free shops
开往	kāi-wǎng	bound for
抵达	dǐ-dá	arrivals
海关	hǎi-guān	customs
站台	zhàn-tái	platform
离境/发车	lí-jìng/fā-chē	departures
询问处	xún-wèn-chù	information
登机口	dēng-jī-kǒu	boarding gate

Hotel/restaurant

衣帽室	yī-mào-shì	cloakroom
冷水	lěng-shuǐ	cold water
热水	rè-shuǐ	hot water
接待处	jiē-dài-chù	reception
紧急出口	jǐn-jí-chū-kǒu	emergency/fire exit

Shops

大减价	dà-jiǎn-jià	sale
开门	kāi-mén	open
关门	guān-mén	closed
收款处	shōu-kuǎn-chù	cashier
电梯	diàn-tī	lift

Sightseeing

儿童票	ér-tóng-piào	child ticket
成人票	chéng-rén-piào	adult ticket
学生票	xué-shēng-piào	student ticket
免费进入	miǎn-fèi jìn-rù	free entry
请勿触摸	qǐng-wù-chù-mō	please don't touch
请勿入内	qǐng-wù-rù-nèi	no entry
请保持安静	qǐng-bǎo-chí-ān-jìng	please keep quiet
禁止拍照	jìn-zhǐ-pāi-zhào	no photography

On the street

电话亭	diàn-huà-tíng	phone box
银行	yín-háng	bank
邮局	yóu-jú	post office
商场	shāng-chǎng	shop
出租车	chū-zū-chē	taxi
餐馆	cān-guǎn	restaurant
旅馆	lǚ-guǎn	hotel
医院	yī-yuàn	hospital
学校	xué-xiào	school
图书馆	tú-shū-guǎn	library
博物馆	bó-wù-guǎn	museum
警察局	jǐng-chá-jú	police station

Reference

Pronouncing place names

. . . .

When travelling around mainland China (中国 zhōng-guó), you will need to bear in mind that place names as we know them are not necessarily the same as in English. Imagine if you needed to buy tickets at a train station but couldn't see your destination on the departures list, or recognise your stop being called out! This handy list eliminates such problems by indicating the pronunciations and characters for major towns and cities.

Beijing	北京	běi-jīng
Chengdu	成都	chéng-dū
Guangzhou	广州	guǎng-zhōu
Hangzhou	杭州	háng-zhōu
Harbin	哈尔滨	hā-ěr-bīn
Nanjing	南京	nán-jīng
Shanghai	上海	shàng-hǎi
Shenzhen	深圳	shēn-zhèn
Suzhou	苏州	sū-zhōu
Tianjin	天津	tiān-jīn
Wuhan	武汉	wǔ-hàn
Xi'an	西安	xī'ān

Grammar

To a certain extent, Mandarin is grammatically simple and straightforward when compared with English and other European languages.

There is no change for verbs in the past tense nor in the past participle, and there are no irregular verbs.

The structure of a question is the same as a statement, but the extra character 吗 (ma) is added at the end.

There is no change for masculine and feminine forms of any Chinese word, unlike in some European languages. However, certain Chinese words are used only for males and certain others only for females; this is equivalent to the example of 'pretty' for females and 'handsome' for males in English.

There is no difference between the singular and plural forms of nouns.

Nouns

• •

A noun is a word such as 'car', 'horse' or 'Mary' which is used to refer to a person or thing.

As in English, nouns in Mandarin are unisex: you don't have to worry about which is masculine and which is feminine. In some European languages, 'apple', for instance, is feminine and 'book' is masculine.

Again, as in English, the article in Mandarin is simple: 这 (zhè) = this, 那 (nà) = that.

To make things even easier, 'the' is not even used in Mandarin!

一 (yī) in Mandarin is equivalent to 'a' or 'an' or 'one' in English.

However, one of the difficult areas of Mandarin is its 'measure words' for nouns. 'Measure words' don't exist in English. For example, you say 'one horse' in English. In Mandarin, you say 'one' + the measure word for 'horse' + 'horse', so we say: 一 匹马 (yī–pī mǎ). There are quite a few different measure words for different nouns. The basic ones are as follows:

个 (gè) is used most frequently. It can be used for person/people, apple and, indeed, most nouns. The good news for anybody who is talking to Chinese people in basic Mandarin, is that you should simply use this measure word for all the nouns if you don't know which measure word is the right one. Chinese people will still understand you.

List of commonly used measure words:

本   (běn) for book, dictionary, magazine

辆   (liàng) for car, bus and train

架   (jià) for plane

匹   (pī) for horse

头   (tóu) for pig, cow, sheep

条   (tiáo) for fish

艘   (sōu) for boat

只   (zhī) for chicken, duck, goose

Pronouns

. . . .

A pronoun is a word that you use to refer to someone or something when you do not need to use a noun, often because the person or thing has been mentioned earlier. Examples are 'it', 'she/he', 'something' and 'myself'.

They are easier in Mandarin than in English; all pronouns in Mandarin stay the same whether they are used as subjects or objects.

Subject	Object	Mandarin pronouns (for both subjects and objects)
I	me	我 (wǒ)
you (singular)	you	你 (nǐ)
you (plural)	you	你们 (nǐ-men)
he	him	他 (tā)
she	her	她 (tā)
it	it	它 (tā)
we	us	我们 (wǒ-men)
they	them	他/她们 (tā-men)
things	them	它们 (tā-men)

Adjectives

An adjective is a word such as 'small', 'pretty' or 'practical' that describes a person or thing, or gives extra information about them.

In Mandarin, adjectives are either in front of or after the noun they describe, for example:

红苹果 (hóng píng-guǒ) (red apple)

苹果是红的 (píng-guǒ shì hóng-de)
(the apple is red)

Please note that 是 (shì) (**to be**) and 的 (de) go before and after the adjective in the second example.

In Mandarin some adjectives are used only to describe men and some are used only to describe women, for example:

英俊的小伙子 (yīng-jùn-de xiǎo huǒ-zi)
(handsome young man)

漂亮的姑娘 (piào-liàng-de gū-niang)
(pretty girl)

My, your, his, her, our, their

• •

In Mandarin, you simply add 的 (de) at the end
of the above pronouns to make them become
adjectives:

my	我的	(wǒ-de)
your (singular)	你的	(nǐ-de)
you (plural)	你们的	(nǐ-men-de)
his	他的	(tā-de)
her	她的	(tā-de)
its	它的	(tā-de)
our	我们的	(wǒ-men-de)
their	他/她们的	(tā-men-de)
things	它们的	(tā-men-de)

Grammar

182

Verbs

· ·

A verb is a word such as 'sing', 'walk' or 'cry' which is used with a subject to say what someone or something does or what happens to them.

In Mandarin, verbs are not divided into regular verbs and irregular verbs, therefore it is easy for beginners to try to build a simple sentence by using a verb: 我喜欢你 (wǒ xǐ-huan nǐ) (I like you).

In Mandarin, the verbs do not have to change when used in the past tense, or as present participles or as past participles. Terms such as 'yesterday' and 'in the past' used before the verb are sufficient to indicate that something happened or has happened. Please note that you normally add 了 (le) after the verb when this verb is being used in the past tense: 我昨天去了伦敦 (wǒ zuó-tiān qù-le-lún-dūn) (I went to London yesterday). Note that in Mandarin you say 'I yesterday go to London'. When using a verb as a present or past participle, you normally add 过 (guò) after the verb: 我去过伦敦 (wǒ qù-guò lún-dūn) (I have/had been to London).

List of commonly used verbs:

吃　(chī) eat

买　(mǎi) buy

卖　(mài) sell

爱　(ài) love

去　(qù) go

喜欢　(xǐ-huan) like

To make a verb negative in Mandarin, you simply insert 不 (bù) before the verb, for example:

我不吃 (wǒ bù-chī) I am not eating

Building basic sentences

As in English, in Chinese there are only a few different structures for basic sentences, as follows:

I am Chinese 我是中国人
wǒ shì zhōng-guó-rén

I like/fancy you 我喜欢你
wǒ xǐ-huan nǐ

Do you like/ 你喜欢我吗?
fancy me? nǐ xǐ-huan wǒ ma?

I have been to 我去过北京
Beijing wǒ qù-guò Běi-jīng

English –
Mandarin
Dictionary

A

a(n)	一	yī
able	可以	kě-yǐ
accelerator	加速器	jiā-sù-qì
to accept	接受	jiē-shòu
accident	事故/意外	shì-gù/yì-wài
accident & emergency department	急诊室	jí-zhěn-shì
accommodation	住处	zhù-chù
address	地址	dì-zhǐ
adult	大人	dà-rén
aeroplane	飞机	fēi-jī
afternoon	下午	xià-wǔ
age	年龄	nián-líng
air conditioning	空调	kōng-tiáo
airport	机场	jī-chǎng
alarm	警报器	jǐng-bào-qì
alcohol	酒	jiǔ

allergic to...	对…过敏	duì... guò-mǐn
alternator	交流发电机	jiāo-liú-fā-diàn-jī
ambulance	救护车	jiù-hù-chē
anaemia	贫血症	pín-xuè-zhèng
anaesthetic	麻醉剂	má-zuì-jì
and	和	hé
another	另外的	lìng-wài-de
antibiotic	抗生素	kàng-shēng-sù
antihistamine	抗组胺剂	kàng-zǔ-ān-jì
antiseptic	杀菌剂	shā-jūn-jì
apple	苹果	píng-guǒ
apricots	杏子	xìng-zi
April	四月	sì-yuè
arm	臂	bì
arrivals (plane, train)	抵达	dǐ-dá
asparagus	芦笋	lú-sǔn
asthma	哮喘病	xiào-chuǎn bìng
aubergine	茄子	qié-zi

August	八月	bā-yuè
Australia	澳大利亚	ào-dà-lì-yà
autumn	秋天	qiū-tiān

B

baby	婴儿/宝宝	yīng-ér/bǎo-bao
bad	坏	huài
bag	包	bāo
baggage reclaim	领取行李	lǐng-qǔ-xíng-li
baker's	面包店	miàn-bāo-diàn
ballet	芭蕾舞	bā-léi-wǔ
banana	香蕉	xiāng-jiāo
bank	银行	yín-háng
banknote	纸币	zhǐ-bì
bar	酒吧	jiǔ-bā
bathroom	浴室	yù-shì
battery (radio, etc.)	电池	diàn-chí
beach	沙滩	shā-tān
beautiful	美丽的	měi-lì-de

bed	床	chuáng
bed (double)	双人床	shuāng-rén-chuáng
bed (single)	单人床	dān-rén-chuáng
bedroom	卧室	wò-shì
beer	啤酒	pí-jiǔ
bicycle	自行车	zì-xíng-chē
big	大	dà
bigger	大些	dà-xiē
bill (hotel, restaurant)	帐单	zhàng-dān
billion	十亿	shí-yì
birthday	生日	shēng-rì
happy birthday!	生日快乐!	shēng-rì-kuài-lè!
my birthday is on...	我的生日是…	wǒ de shēng-rì shì...
birthday card	生日贺卡	shēng-rì hè-kǎ
birthday present	生日礼物	shēng-rì lǐ-wù
biscuits	饼干	bǐng-gān
a bit	一点	yī-diǎn

191

bitter (taste)	苦	kǔ
black	黑色	hēi-sè
bleach	去污液	qù-wū-yè
blood	血	xuè
blood pressure	血压	xuè-yā
high/low blood pressure	高/低血压	gāo/dī-xuè-yā
blouse	女衬衫	nǚ chèn-shān
blue (light)	蓝色的	lán-sè-de
boarding gate	登机口	dēng-jī-kǒu
body	身体	shēn-tǐ
bonnet (of car)	发动机罩盖	fā-dòng-jī-zhào-gài
book	书	shū
bookshop	书店	shū-diàn
boots (long)	长靴子	cháng xuē-zi
boots (ankle)	短靴子	duǎn xuē-zi
bottle	瓶	píng
bottle of wine	一瓶葡萄酒	yī píng pú-táo-jiǔ

bowl	碗	wǎn
box (theatre)	包厢	bāo-xiāng
box office	售票处	shòu-piào-chù
boy (young child)	男孩	nán-hái
boyfriend	男朋友	nán-péng-yǒu
brakes	刹车闸	shā-chē-zhá
brand (make)	品牌	pǐn-pái
brandy	白兰地	bái-lán-dì
bread	面包	miàn-bāo
breakfast	早餐	zǎo-cān
breathing difficulties	呼吸困难	hū-xī-kùn-nán
bride	新娘	xīn-niáng
bridegroom	新郎	xīn-láng
briefcase	手提箱	shǒu-tí-xiāng
Britain	英国	yīng-guó
British	英国的	yīng-guó-de
brochure	小册子	xiǎo-cè-zi
bronchitis	支气管炎	zhī-qì-guǎn-yán

B

brother	兄弟	xiōng-dì
brown	棕色	zōng-sè
bulb (lightbulb)	灯泡	dēng-pào
bureau de change	兑换处	duì-huàn-chù
burger	汉堡包	hàn-bǎo-bāo
burglar	盗窃犯	dào-qiè-fàn
bus	公共汽车	gōng-gòng-qì-chē
bus station	公共汽车站	gōng-gòng-qì-chē-zhàn
bus stop	公共汽车站	gōng-gòng-qì-chē-zhàn
bus ticket	公共汽车车票	gōng-gòng-qì-chē chē-piào
business	公务	shāng-wù
business trip	公差	gōng-chāi
butcher's	肉店	ròu-diàn
butter	黄油	huáng-yóu
by (next to)	邻近	lín-jìn
by bus	乘坐公共汽车	chéng-zuò gōng-gòng-qì-chē

| by car | 坐轿车 | zuò jiào-chē |
| by train | 坐火车 | zuò huǒ-chē |

C

cab (taxi)	出租车	chū-zū-chē
café	咖啡吧	kā-fēi-bā
cake	蛋糕	dàn-gāo
cake shop	蛋糕店	dàn-gāo-diàn
call (phonecall)	打 (电话)	dǎ (diàn-huà)
calligraphy	书法	shū-fǎ
camera	相机	xiàng-jī
campsite	野营地	yě-yíng-dì
can (to be able)	可以/能	kě-yǐ/néng
can I...?	我可以/能…吗?	wǒ kě-yǐ/néng… ma?
can we...?	我们可以/能…吗?	wǒ-men kě-yǐ/néng… ma?
Canada	加拿大	jiā-ná-dà
Cantonese (language)	广东话	guǎng-dōng-huà

capital (city)	首都	shǒu-dū
car	轿车	jiào-chē
carrots	胡萝卜	hú-luó-bo
cartoons	卡通片	kǎ-tōng-piàn
cash	现金	xiàn-jīn
to cash (cheque)	兑现 (支票)	duì-xiàn (zhī-piào)
cash desk	现金柜台	xiàn-jīn-guì-tái
cash machine	取钞机	qǔ-chāo-jī
cashier	收款处	shōu-kuǎn-chù
casualty department	急诊部	jí-zhěn-bù
cat	猫	māo
cauliflower	菜花	cài-huā
caution	小心	xiǎoxīn
CD	光碟	guāng-dié
celery	芹菜	qín-cài
chair	椅子	yǐ-zi
to change (money)	换 (钱)	huàn (qián)
charge (fee)	收费	shōu-fèi

to charge (mobile, etc.)	充电	chōng-diàn
cheap	便宜的	pián-yì-de
to check in (airport/hotel)	办理登机／入住手续	bàn-lǐ dēng-jī/rù-zhù shǒu-xù
cheers!	干杯！	gān-bēi!
cheese	奶酪	nǎi-lào
chemist's	药店	yào-diàn
cheque	支票	zhī-piào
cherries	樱桃	yīng-táo
chest	胸腔	xiōng-qiāng
chicken	鸡	jī
chicken breast	鸡胸肉	jī-xiōng ròu
child	孩子	hái-zi
children	孩子们	hái-zi-men
chilli	辣椒	là-jiāo
China	中国	zhōng-guó
Chinese (language)	汉语	hàn-yǔ
Chinese (person)	中国人	zhōng-guó-rén

Chinese tea	中国茶	zhōng-guó-chá
chips (french fries)	炸薯条	zhá-shǔ-tiáo
chocolate	巧克力	qiǎo-kè-lì
choke (car)	阻风门	zǔ-fēng-mén
chopsticks	筷子	kuài-zi
Christmas	圣诞节	shèng-dàn-jié
Merry Christmas!	圣诞快乐!	shèng-dàn kuài-lè!
church	教堂	jiào-táng
cigarette	香烟	xiāng-yān
cigarette lighter	打火机	dǎ-huǒ-jī
cinema	电影院	diàn-yǐng-yuàn
circle (theatre)	半圆形楼座	bàn-yuán-xǐng-lóu-zuò
city	城市	chéng-shì
cloakroom	衣帽间	yī-mào-jiān
clock	闹钟	nào-zhōng
Cloisonné	景泰蓝	jǐng-tài-lán
close	关门	guān-mén

clothes	衣服	yī-fu
cloudy	多云	duō-yún
clutch (car)	离合器	lí-hé-qì
coach	长途客车	cháng-tú-kè-chē
coat	大衣	dà-yī
cocktail	鸡尾酒	jī-wěi-jiǔ
coffee	咖啡	kā-fēi
coffee (black)	咖啡不加奶	kā-fēi bù jiā-nǎi
coffee (instant)	速溶咖啡	sù-róng kā-fēi
coffee (white)	咖啡加奶	kā-fēi jiā-nǎi
coin	硬币	yìng-bì
Coke®	可乐	kě-lè
cold	冷的	lěng-de
I have a cold	我感冒了	wǒ gǎn-mào-le
cold water	冷水	lěng-shuǐ
colleague	同事	tóng-shì
come in!	请进!	qǐng-jìn!
complaint	投诉	tóu-sù

computer	电脑	diàn-nǎo
concert	音乐会	yīn-yuè-huì
condoms	避孕套	bì-yùn-tào
conference	会议	huì-yì
congratulations	祝贺/恭喜	zhù-hè/gōng-xǐ
contract	合同	hé-tong
copy (verb/noun)	复印/ 复印件	fù-yìn/fù-yìn-jiàn
corner (of road)	(路)边	(lù)-biān
cosmetics	化妆品	huà-zhuāng-pǐn
country (nation)	国家	guó-jiā
cream	奶油	nǎi-yóu
credit card	信用卡	xìn-yòng-kǎ
crisps	薯片	shǔ-piàn
crossroads	十字路口	shí-zì-lù-kǒu
cucumber	黄瓜	huáng-guā
customs (duty)	海关	hǎi-guān

danger	危险	wēi-xiǎn
date	日期	rì-qī
date of birth	生日	shēng-rì
daughter	女儿	nǔ-ér
daughter-in-law	儿媳妇	ér-xí-fù
dear	亲爱的	qīn-ài-de
December	十二月	shí-èr-yuè
delay	延误	yán-wù
delay (on train notice boards)	误点	wù-diǎn
dentist	牙医	yá-yī
department store	百货商店	bǎi-huò-shāng-diàn
departure lounge	候机厅	hòu-jī-tīng
departures	起飞	qǐ-fēi
deposit	定金	dìng-jīn
dessert	甜品	tián-pǐn
diabetes	糖尿病	táng-nìao-bìng

diabetic	患糖尿病	huàn táng-niào-bìng
I'm diabetic	我是糖尿病患者	wǒ shì táng-niào-bìng huàn-zhě
dictionary	字典	zì-diǎn
diesel	柴油	chái-yóu
diet	节食	jié-shí
digital camera	数码相机	shù-mǎ xiàng-jī
dining room	餐厅	cān-tīng
dinner (evening meal)	晚餐	wǎn-cān
directions	方向	fāng-xiàng
directory (telephone)	电话簿	diàn-huà-bù
dirty	肮脏的	āng-zāng-de
disabled (person)	残疾人	cán-jí-rén
discount	折扣	zhé-kòu
distributor (as part of car)	分销商	fēn-xiāo-shāng
divorced	离婚了	lí-hūn le
doctor	医生	yī-shēng
documents	文件	wén-jiàn

dog	狗	gǒu
domestic (flights)	国内的	guó-nèi-de
door	门	mén
double	双人	shuāng-rén
double bed	双人床	shuāng-rén-chuáng
double room	双人房	shuāng-rén-fáng
down	下	xià
downstairs	楼下	lóu-xià
dress	连衣裙	lián-yī-qún
drink (soft)	饮料	yǐn-liào
drinking water	饮用水	yǐn-yòng-shuǐ
driver (of car)	司机	sī-jī
driving licence	驾驶证	jià-shǐ-zhèng
drug (medicine)	药	yào
drug (narcotics)	毒品	dú-pǐn
dry-cleaner's	干洗店	gān-xǐ-diàn
duty-free	免税	miǎn-shuì
duty-free shops	免税店	miǎn-shuì-diàn

203

E

earphones	耳机	ěr-jī
Easter	复活节	fù-huó-jié
egg	蛋	dàn
eight	八	bā
eighteen	十八	shí-bā
eighth	第八	dì-bā
eighty	八十	bā-shí
electric socket	电源	diàn-yuán
electricity	电	diàn
eleven	十一	shí-yī
e-mail	电子邮件	diàn-zǐ-yóu-jiàn
embassy	大使馆	dà-shǐ-guǎn
emergency	紧急事件	jǐn-jí-shì-jiàn
emergency exit	紧急出口	jǐn-jí-chū-kǒu
engine	发动机	fā-dòng-jī
England	英格兰	yīng-gé-lán
English (person)	英国人	yīng-guó-rén

English (language)	英语	yīng-yǔ
entrance	入口	rù-kǒu
entrance fee	入场费	rù-chǎng-fèi
equipment	设备	shè-bèi
Europe	欧洲	ōu-zhōu
evening	晚上	wǎn-shàng
this evening	今晚	jīn-wǎn
tomorrow evening	明晚	míng-wǎn
exchange rate	兑换率	duì-huàn-lǜ
excuse me! (sorry)	对不起！	duì-bù-qǐ!
excuse me! (when passing)	请让一让！	qǐng ràng-yī-ràng!
exhaust (car)	废气	fèi-qì
exhibition	展览	zhǎn-lǎn
exit	出口	chū-kǒu
expensive	昂贵的	áng-guì-de
eye	眼睛	yǎn-jīng

F

face	脸	liǎn
family	家庭	jiā-tíng
father	父亲	fù-qin
fax	传真	chuán-zhēn
February	二月	èr-yuè
feet	脚	jiǎo
female	女的	nǚ-de
fever	发烧	fā-shāo
fiancé(e)	未婚夫/妻	wèi-hūn-fū/qī
fifteen	十五	shí-wǔ
fifth	第五	dì-wǔ
fifty	五十	wǔ-shí
film (at cinema)	电影	diàn-yǐng
finger	手指	shǒu-zhǐ
fire	火	huǒ
fire!	着火了!	zháo-huǒ-le!
fire alarm	火警报警器	huǒ-jǐng bào-jǐng-qì

fire brigade	消防队	xiāo-fáng-duì
fire escape	太平梯	tài-píng-tī
fire extinguisher	灭火器	miè-huǒ-qì
firemen	消防员	xiāo-fáng-yuán
first	第一	dì-yī
first aid	急救	jí-jiù
first class	一等舱／一等 车厢	yī-děng-cāng／ yī-děng-chē-xiāng
fish	鱼	yú
five	五	wǔ
flight	航班	háng-bān
flour	面粉	miàn-fěn
flowers	花	huā
flu	流感	liú-gǎn
fog	雾	wù
food	食物	shí-wù
food poisoning	食物中毒	shí-wù-zhòng-dú
foot	脚	jiǎo
football	足球	zú-qiú

foreigner	外国人	wài-guó-rén
fork (cutlery)	叉	chā
forty	四十	sì-shí
fountain	喷泉	pēn-quán
four	四	sì
fourteen	十四	shí-sì
fourth	第四	dì-sì
France	法国	fǎ-guó
French (language)	法语	fǎ-yǔ
French (person)	法国人	fǎ-guó-rén
Friday	星期五	xīng-qī-wǔ
friend	朋友	péng-yǒu
fruit	水果	shuǐ-guǒ
fruit juice	果汁	guǒ-zhī
fruit shop	水果店	shuǐ-guǒ-diàn
fuse	保险丝	bǎo-xiǎn-sī

gallery	美术馆	měi-shù-guǎn
garage	修车行	xiū-chē-háng
garden	花园	huā-yuán
garlic	大蒜	dà-suàn
gate (airport)	登机口	dēng-jī-kǒu
gears	换档	huàn-dǎng
gents' (toilet)	男厕所	nán-cè-suǒ
German (language)	德语	dé-yǔ
German (person)	德国人	dé-guó-rén
Germany	德国	dé-guó
gift	礼物	lǐ-wù
gift shop	礼品店	lǐ-pǐn-diàn
girl	女孩	nǚ-hái
girlfriend	女朋友	nǚ-péng-yǒu
glass (substance)	玻璃	bō-li
glass (for drinking)	玻璃杯	bō-li-bēi
a glass of water	一杯水	yī bēi shuǐ

a glass of wine	一杯葡萄酒	yī bēi pú-tao-jiǔ
to go	去	qù
I'm going to...	我正要去…	wǒ zhèng yào qù...
we're going to...	我们正要去…	wǒ men zhèng yào qù...
good	好	hǎo
goodbye	再见	zài-jiàn
goodnight	晚安	wǎn-ān
gram	克	kè
grapefruit	葡萄柚	pú-tao-yòu
grapes	葡萄	pú-tao
green (colour)	绿色	lǜ-sè
green tea	绿茶	lǜ-chá
grey	灰色	huī-sè
grocer's	杂货店	zá-huò-diàn
ground floor	一楼	yī lóu
guide (tourist)	导游	dǎo-yóu
guidebook	导游册	dǎo-yóu-cè
guided tour	有导游的游览	yǒu dǎo-yóu de yóu-lǎn

hair	头发	tóu-fa
hairdresser's	美发师	měi-fà-shī
half	一半	yī-bàn
half-price	半价	bàn-jià
hamburger	汉堡包	hàn-bǎo-bāo
hand	手	shǒu
handbag	手提包	shǒu-tí-bāo
handbrake	手刹	shǒu-shā
handicapped	有残疾	yǒu-cán-jí
hand luggage	手提行李	shǒu-tí xíng-li
happy	快乐	kuài-lè
happy anniversary!	纪念日快乐！	jì-niàn-rì kuài-lè!
happy birthday!	生日快乐！	shēng-rì kuài-lè!
happy Easter!	复活节快乐！	fù-huó-jié kuài-lè!
happy New Year!	新年快乐！	xīn-nián kuài- lè!
to have	有	yǒu
I have...	我有…	wǒ yǒu...

we have...	我们有…	wǒ-men yǒu...
he	他	tā
head	头	tóu
headache	头疼	tóu-téng
headlights	车头灯	chē-tóu-dēng
heart	心	xīn
heartbeat	心跳	xīn-tìao
heart disease	心脏病	xīn-zàng-bìng
heating	暖气	nuǎn-qì
hello	你好	nǐ-hǎo
to help	帮助	bāng-zhù
help!	救命啊!	jiù-mìng a!
can you help me?	你能帮助我吗?	nǐ néng bāng-zhù wǒ ma?
her	她的	tā-de
here is...	这里是…	zhè-lǐ shì...
here is my passport	这是我的护照	zhè shì wǒ de hù-zhào
him	他	tā

hire (car)	租借车	zū-jiè-chē
his	他的	tā-de
holiday	度假	dù-jià
home	家	jiā
hospital	医院	yī-yuàn
hot	热	rè
hot water	热水	rè-shuǐ
hotel	旅馆	lǚ-guǎn
how are you?	你好吗?	nǐ hǎo ma?
how much is it?	多少钱?	duō-shǎo qián?
hungry	饿	è

I

I	我	wǒ
ice	冰	bīng
ice-cream	冰淇淋	bīng-qí-lín
ice-lolly	冰棍	bīng-gùn
identity card	身份证	shēn-fèn-zhèng

ignition	点火	diǎn-huǒ
ill	生病	shēng-bìng
I'm ill	我病了	wǒ bìng-le
indicator	显示器	xiǎn-shì-qì
infection	炎症	yán-zhèng
information	资讯	zī-xùn
insurance	保险	bǎo-xiǎn
fully comprehensive insurance	全保险	quán bǎo-xiǎn
international	国际的	guó-jì-de
invitation	邀请	yāo-qǐng
Ireland	爱尔兰	ài-ěr-lán
iron (for clothes)	熨斗	yùn-dǒu
island	岛	dǎo
Italian (language)	意大利语	yì-dà-lì-yǔ
Italian (person)	意大利人	yì-dà-lì-rén
Italy	意大利	yì-dà-lì

J

jacket	夹克衫	jiá-kè-shān
jade	玉石	yù-shí
jam (food)	果酱	guǒ-jiàng
January	一月	yī-yuè
jeweller's	珠宝店	zhū-bǎo-diàn
jewellery	珠宝	zhū-bǎo
Jewish	犹太人	yóu-tài-rén
job	工作	gōng-zuò
to joke	开玩笑	kāi-wán-xiào
journalist	记者	jì-zhě
journey	旅程	lǚ-chéng
July	七月	qī-yuè
jumper	毛衣	máo-yī
June	六月	liù-yuè

K

| keep out | 止步 | zhǐ-bù |
| key | 钥匙 | yào-shi |

L

kilogram	公斤	gōng-jīn
kilometre	公里	gōng-lǐ
kind (person)	友善的	yǒu-shàn-de
kiosk	收银处	shōu-yín-chù
knickers	女内裤	nǚ nèi-kù
to knock (on door)	敲 (门)	qiāo (mén)
to know (facts)	知道	zhī-dào
I don't know	我不知道	wǒ bù zhī-dào

L

ladies (toilet)	女厕所	nǚ-cè-suǒ
lady	女士	nǚ-shì
lamp	台灯	tái-dēng
language	语言	yǔ-yán
large	大	dà
left (not right)	左	zuǒ
left-luggage	行李暂存	xíng-li zàn-cún
leg	腿	tuǐ
lemon	柠檬	níng-méng

lemonade	七喜	qī-xǐ
less	更小的	gèng-xiǎo-de
letter	信	xìn
library	图书馆	tú-shū-guǎn
licence (driving)	驾驶证	jià-shǐ-zhèng
lift (elevator)	电梯	diàn-tī
light	灯	dēng
to like	喜欢	xǐ-huan
I like coffee	我喜欢咖啡	wǒ xǐ-huan kā-fēi
I'd like...	我想…	wǒ xiǎng...
I don't like...	我不喜欢…	wǒ bù xǐ-huan...
We'd like...	我们想…	wǒ-men xiǎng...
liqueur	烈酒	liè-jiǔ
litre	升	shēng
a little...	一点…	yī-diǎn...
to live in...	住在…	zhù-zài...
I live in London	我住在伦敦…	wǒ zhù-zài-lún-dūn...
long	长的	cháng-de

217

to lose	丢失	diū-shī
I've lost my...	我丢失了我的···	wǒ diū-shī-le wǒ-de...
lost property office	失物认领处	shī-wù rèn-lǐng-chù
love	爱	ài
luggage	行李	xíng-li
luggage trolley	行李手推车	xíng-li-shǒu-tuī-chē
lunch	午饭	wǔ-fàn

M

Madam/Ms...	女士···	nǚ-shì...
magazine	杂志	zá-zhì
male	男的	nán-de
man	男人	nán-rén
manager	经理	jīng-lǐ
Mandarin (language)	普通话	pǔ-tōng-huà
map (of country)	地图	dì-tú
March	三月	sān-yuè

married	结婚了	jié-hūn le
I'm married	我已经结婚了	wǒ yǐ-jīng-jié-hūn le
are you married?	你结婚了吗?	nǐ jié-hūn le ma?
May	五月	wǔ-yuè
meal	饭	fàn
meat	肉	ròu
medicine	药	yào
meet	会面	huì-miàn
pleased to meet you!	幸会!	xìng-huì!
melon	瓜	guā
menu	菜单	cài-dān
message	留言	liú-yán
metro (underground)	地铁	dì-tiě
metro station	地铁站	dì-tiě-zhàn
military police	军警	jūn-jǐng
milk	牛奶	niú-nǎi
million	一百万	yī-bǎi-wàn

mind: *do you mind?*	你介意吗?	nǐ jiè-yì ma?
I don't mind	我不介意	wǒ bù jiè-yì
mineral water	矿泉水	kuàng-quán-shuǐ
Ming porcelain	明瓷器	míng-cí-qì
minute	分钟	fēn-zhōng
Miss...	…小姐	…xiǎo- jiě
to miss (train, etc.)	误了	wù-le
mistake	错误	cuò-wù
mobile number	手机号码	shǒu-jī hào-mǎ
mobile phone	手机	shǒu-jī
Monday	星期一	xīng-qī-yī
money	钱	qián
I have no money	我没有钱	wǒ méi-yǒu qián
month	月	yuè
monthly	每月	měi-yuè
more	更多的	gèng-duō-de
some more...	更多的	gèng-duō-de
morning	早晨	zǎo-chén

mother	母亲	mǔ-qīn
motorway	高速公路	gāo-sù-gōng-lù
mouth	嘴	zuǐ
movie	电影	diàn-yǐng
Mr...	…先生	…xiān-sheng
Mrs...	…太太	…tài-tai
mugging	抢劫	qiǎng-jié
museum	博物馆	bó-wù-guǎn
mushrooms	蘑菇	mó-gu
music	音乐	yīn-yuè
musical production	歌剧	gē-jù
my	我的	wǒ-de

N

name	名字	míng-zi
my name is...	我的名字是…	wǒ-de míng-zi shì...
what is your name?	你叫什么名字?	nǐ jiào shén-me míng-zi?

nationality	国籍	guó-jí
near to...	靠近…	kào-jìn...
need: *I need...*	我需要…	wǒ xū-yào...
we need...	我们需要…	wǒ-men xū-yào...
new	新的	xīn-de
New Year	新年	xīn-nián
happy New Year!	新年快乐!	xīn-nián-kuài-lè!
New Zealand	新西兰	xīn-xī-lán
news	新闻	xīn-wén
newsagent	报摊	bào-tān
newspaper	报纸	bào-zhǐ
next to	旁边的	páng-biān-de
nine	九	jiǔ
nineteen	十九	shí-jiǔ
nineteenth	第九	dì-jiǔ
ninety	九十	jiǔ-shí
no	不	bù
no entry	不许进入	bù-xǔ jìn-rù

no photography	禁止拍照	jìn-zhǐ-pāi-zhào
no smoking	不许抽烟	bù-xǔ chōu-yān
no swimming	禁止游泳	jìn-zhǐ-yóu-yǒng
no, thanks	不，谢谢	bù, xiè-xie
noise	噪音	zào-yīn
Northern Ireland	北爱尔兰	běi-ài-ér-lán
nose	鼻子	bí-zi
not	不	bù
novel	小说	xiǎo-shuō
number	号码	hào-mǎ

O

oats	麦片	mài-piàn
occupied	有人	yǒu-rén
October	十月	shí-yuè
office	办公室	bàn-gōng-shì
OK!	好！	hǎo!
old (not young)	老（不年轻）	lǎo (bù nián-qīng)

how old are you?	你多大年纪了?	nǐ duō-dà nián-jì-le?
I'm... years old	我···岁了	wǒ... suì-le
olive oil	橄榄油	gǎn-lán-yǒu
at once	马上	mǎ-shàng
one	一	yī
one hundred	一百	yī-bǎi
onions	洋葱	yáng-cōng
open	打开	dǎ-kāi
opposite	对面的	duì-miàn-de
optician	眼镜商	yǎn-jìng-shāng
orange (colour)	橙色	chéng-sè
orange (fruit)	橙子	chéng-zi
orange juice	橙汁	chéng-zhī
freshly squeezed orange juice	鲜榨橙汁	xiān-zhà-chéng-zhī
our	我们的	wǒ-men-de
owe: I owe you...	我欠你···	wǒ qiàn nǐ...
you owe me...	你欠我···	nǐ qiàn wǒ...

package	包裹	bāo-guǒ
pain	疼痛	téng-tòng
painting (picture)	画	huà
pair	双/对	shuāng/duì
palace	宫殿	gōng-diàn
paper	纸	zhǐ
pardon?	您说什么？	nín shuō shén-me?
I beg your pardon?	请您再说一遍？	qǐng nín zài shuō yī-biàn?
parents	父母	fù-mǔ
park	公园	gōng-yuán
to park	停车	tíng-chē
partner (business)	伙伴	huǒ-bàn
partner (boyfriend/ girlfriend)	伴侣	bàn-lǚ
party (celebration)	晚会	wǎn-huì
passenger	旅客	lǚ-kè
passport	护照	hù-zhào

to pay	支付	zhī-fù
I want to pay	我想付款	wǒ xiǎng fù-kuǎn
where do I pay?	我在哪里付款?	wǒ zài nǎ-lǐ fù-kuǎn?
payment	付款	fù-kuǎn
peaches	桃子	táo-zi
peanut allergy	对花生过敏	duì huā-shēng guò-mǐn
pears	梨	lí
peas	豌豆	wān-dòu
pen	笔	bǐ
people	人们	rén-men
pepper (spice)	胡椒	hú-jiāo
pepper (vegetable)	青椒	qīng-jiāo
perfume shop	香水店	xiāng-shuǐ-diàn
person	人	rén
petrol	汽油	qì-yóu
petrol station	加油站	jiā-yóu-zhàn
pharmacy	药店	yào-diàn

phone	电话	diàn-huà
phone box	电话亭	diàn-huà-tíng
phonecard	电话卡	diàn-huà-kǎ
photograph	相片	xiàng-piàn
photographic shop	相馆	xiàng-guǎn
phrasebook	短语集	duǎn-yǔ-jí
pillow	枕头	zhěn-tou
pink	粉红色	fěn-hóng-sè
pity: *what a pity!*	真可惜！	zhēn-kě-xī!
place	地方	dì-fāng
place of birth	出生地	chū-shēng-dì
plane	飞机	fēi-jī
plate	碟子	dié-zi
platform (railway)	站台	zhàn-tái
play (theatre)	演出	yǎn-chū
please	请	qǐng
yes, please	好，谢谢	hǎo, xiè-xie

pleased to meet you	认识你很高兴	rèn-shi nǐ hěn-gāo-xìng
plums	李子	lǐ-zi
poisonous	有毒的	yǒu-dú-de
police	警察	jǐng-chá
police station	警察局	jǐng-chá-jú
pool (swimming)	游泳池	yóu-yǒng-chí
pork	猪肉	zhū-ròu
porter (for luggage)	行李搬运工	xíng-li bān-yùn-gōng
Portugal	葡萄牙	pú-táo-yá
Portuguese (language)	葡萄牙语	pú-táo-yá-yǔ
Portuguese (people)	葡萄牙人	pú-táo-yá-rén
postbox	邮箱	yóu-xiāng
postcard	明信片	míng-xìn-piàn
postcode	邮政编码	yóu-zhèng-biān-mǎ
post office	邮电局	yóu-diàn-jú
potato	土豆	tǔ-dòu

present (gift)	礼物	lǐ-wù
price	价格	jià-gé
private facilities	私人设施	sī-rěn-shè-shī
problem	问题	wèn-tí
to pronounce	发音	fā-yīn
public holiday	公共假期	gōng-gòng jià-qi
to pull	拉	lā
purse	钱包	qián-bāo
to push	推	tuī
pyjamas	睡衣	shuì-yī

Q

quality	质量	zhì-liàng
quantity	数量	shù-liàng
to quarrel	争吵	zhēng-chǎo
queue	排队	pái-duì
quickly	快点	kuài-diǎn
quiet (place)	安静	ān-jìng

race (sport)	赛跑	sài-pǎo
racket (tennis, etc.)	球拍	qiú-pāi
radiator	散热器	sàn-rè-qì
radio	收音机	shōu-yīn-jī
railway station	火车站	huǒ-chē-zhàn
rain	雨	yǔ
to rain	下雨	xià-yǔ
raincoat	雨衣	yǔ-yī
raped	被强奸	bèi-qiáng-jiān
rate of exchange	兑换率	duì-huàn-lǜ
receipt	收据	shōu-jù
reception (desk)	接待处	jiē-dài-chù
receptionist	接待员	jiē-dài-yuán
red	红色的	hóng-sè-de
reduction	折扣	zhé-kòu
refund	退款	tuì-kuǎn
register	注册	zhù-cè
registration form	注册表格	zhù-cè-biǎo-gé

remote control	遥控	yáo-kòng
repair	修理	xiū-lǐ
to reserve	预定	yù-dìng
to rest	休息	xiū-xi
restaurant	餐馆	cān-guǎn
retired: *I'm retired*	我退休了	wǒ tuì-xiū le
return ticket	往返票	wǎng-fǎn-piào
reverse gear	倒车档	dào-chē-dǎng
rice	大米	dà-mǐ
right (not left)	右	yòu
road	公路	gōng-lù
road map	公路地图	gōng-lù dì-tú
road sign	路标	lù-biāo
room (hotel)	客房	kè-fáng
room (double)	双人房	shuāng-rén-fáng
room (single)	单人房	dān-rén-fáng
rose	玫瑰	méi-guī
rubbish	垃圾	lā-jī

safe (for valuables)	保险柜	bǎo-xiǎn-guì
safe (medicine, etc.)	安全的	ān-quán-de
safety	安全	ān-quán
salad	凉拌菜	liáng-bàn-cài
sale	廉售	lián-shòu
salesman/ woman	销售员	xiāo-shòu-yuán
salt	盐	yán
sand	沙	shā
sandwich	三明治	sān-míng-zhì
satellite TV	卫星电视	wèi-xīng diàn-shì
Saturday	星期六	xīng-qī-liù
school	学校	xué-xiào
Scotland	苏格兰	sū-gé-lán
Scottish	苏格兰人	sū-gé-lán-rén
sea	大海	dà-hǎi
seafood	海鲜	hǎi-xiān

seaside: *at the seaside*	在海边	zài-hǎi-biān
season (of year)	季节	jì-jié
seat (chair)	座位	zuò-wèi
seatbelt	安全带	ān-quán-dài
second	第二	dì-èr
to see	看	kàn
see you later	一会儿见	yī huìr jiàn
see you tomorrow	明天见	míng tiān jiàn
to sell	卖	mài
do you sell...?	你们卖…吗?	nǐ-men mài...ma?
September	九月	jiǔ-yuè
series/soap (TV)	连续剧	lián-xù-jù
service charge	服务费	fú-wù-fèi
set menu	套餐菜单	tào-cān cài-dān
seven	七	qī
seventeen	十七	shí-qī
seventh	第七	dì-qī
seventy	七十	qī-shí

233

she	她	tā
sheet (bed)	床单	chuáng-dān
shirt	衬衫	chèn-shān
shoe	鞋	xié
shoe shop	鞋店	xié-diàn
shop	商店	shāng-diàn
shorts	短裤	duǎn-kù
shoulder	肩膀	jiān-bǎng
sightseeing tour	观光游览	guān-guāng-yóu-lǎn
signature	签名	qiān-míng
silk	丝绸	sī-chóu
silk dress	真丝连衣裙	zhēn-sī-lían-yī-qún
silk scarf	丝巾	sī-jīn
silk tie	真丝领带	zhēn-sī-lǐng-dài
silver	银	yín
single (unmarried)	单身的	dān-shēn-de
single bed	单人床	dān-rén-chuáng

single room	单人房	dān-rén-fáng
Sir	先生	xiān-sheng
sister	姐妹	jiě-mèi
to sit	坐下	zuò-xià
please, sit down	请坐下	qǐng-zuò-xià
six	六	liù
sixteen	十六	shí-liù
sixth	第六	dì-liù
sixty	六十	liù-shí
ski pass	滑雪通票	huá-xuě-tōng-piào
skin	皮肤	pí-fū
skirt	短裙	duǎn-qún
skis	雪橇	xuě-qiāo
sky	天	tiān
to sleep	睡觉	shuì-jiào
small	小	xiǎo
smaller	小些其它颜色	xiǎo-xiē
smoke: *to smoke*	抽烟	chōu-yān

I don't smoke	我不抽烟	wǒ bù chōu-yān
may I smoke?	我能抽烟吗?	wǒ néng chōu-yān ma?
snow	雪	xuě
to snow: *it's snowing*	正在下雪	zhèng-zài xià-xuě
soap	肥皂	féi-zào
soap powder	洗衣粉	xǐ-yī-fěn
socks	短袜	duǎn-wà
sofa	沙发	shā-fā
soft drink	软饮料	ruǎn-yǐn-liào
son	儿子	ér-zi
song	歌	gē
sore throat	喉咙疼	hóu-lóng-téng
sorry: *I'm sorry!*	对不起!	duì-bù-qǐ!
soup	汤	tāng
souvenir	礼品	lǐ-pǐn
soya sauce	酱油	jiàng-yóu
Spain	西班牙	xī-bān-yá
Spanish (language)	西班牙语	xī-bān-yá-yǔ

Spanish (people)	西班牙人	xī-bān-yá-rén
spark plug	火花塞	huǒ-huā-sāi
spatula	锅铲	guō-chǎn
to speak	说	shuō
I don't speak Mandarin	我不会说普通话	wǒ bù huì shuō pǔ-tōng-huà
do you speak English?	你说英文吗?	nǐ shuō yīng-wén ma?
speeding	超速	chāo-sù
speed limit	速度限制	sù-dù xiàn-zhì
spinach	菠菜	bō-cài
spirits (alcohol)	酒	jiǔ
spoon	勺子	sháo-zi
sports shop	体育用品商店	tǐ-yù-yòng-pǐn shāng-diàn
spring (season)	春天	chūn-tiān
square (in town)	广场	guǎng-chǎng
staff	员工	yuán-gōng
stalls (theatre)	正厅前排	zhèng-tīng-qián-pái

stamp	邮票	yóu-piào
start	开始	kāi-shǐ
starter (food)	头盘	tóu-pán
station	车站	chē-zhàn
bus station	公共汽车站	gōng-gòng-qì-chē-zhàn
railway station	火车站	huǒ-chē-zhàn
underground station	地铁站	dì-tiě-zhàn
to stay (remain)	住	zhù
I'm staying at...	我住在…	wǒ zhù-zài...
to steal	偷	tōu
steering	转向	zhuǎn-xiàng
steering wheel	方向盘	fāng-xiàng-pán
stomach	胃	wèi
stomach ache	胃疼	wèi-téng
stone	石头	shí-tou
to stop (come to a halt)	停止	tíng-zhǐ
store	商场	shāng-chǎng

straight on	一直往前走	yī-zhí wǎng-qián-zǒu
strawberries	草莓	cǎo-méi
street	街道	jiē-dào
street map	街道地图	jiē-dào dì-tú
student	学生	xué-shēng
sugar	糖	táng
suit	西装	xī-zhuāng
suitcase	手提箱	shǒu-tí-xiāng
summer	夏天	xià-tiān
sun	太阳	tài-yáng
to sunbathe	日光浴	rì-guāng-yù
sunblock	防晒油	fáng-shài-yóu
Sunday	星期日	xīng-qī-rì
sunglasses	太阳镜	tài-yáng-jìng
supermarket	超市	chāo-shì
supper (dinner)	晚餐	wǎn-cān
surname	姓	xìng
my surname is...	我姓…	wǒ-xìng...

swimming pool	游泳池	yóu-yǒng-chí
swimsuit	游泳衣	yóu-yǒng-yī
Swiss (language)	瑞士语	ruì-shì-yǔ
Swiss (people)	瑞士人	ruì-shì-rén
to switch off	关	guān
to switch on	开	kāi
Switzerland	瑞士	ruì-shì

T

t-shirt	T恤衫	t-xù-shān
table	桌子	zhuō-zi
table tennis	网球	wǎng-qiú
tablet (pill)	药丸	yào-wán
Tang poetry	唐诗	táng-shī
taxi	出租车	chū-zū-chē
tea	茶	chá
Chinese green tea	中国绿茶	zhōng-guó-lǜ-chá
green tea	绿茶	lǜ-chá

red tea	红	hóng
teacher	教师	jiào-shī
teeth	牙	yá
telephone	电话	diàn-huà
to telephone	打电话	dǎ diàn-huà
telephone box	电话亭	diàn-huà-tíng
telephone number	电话号码	diàn-huà hào-mǎ
television	电视	diàn-shì
to tell	告诉	gào-sù
temperature	温度	wēn-dù
to have a temperature	发烧	fā-shāo
ten	十	shí
tenth	第十	dì-shí
tennis	网球	wǎng-qiú
terracotta	兵马俑	bīng-mǎ-yǒng
thank you	谢谢您	xiè-xie-nín
no, thanks	不, 谢谢	bù, xiè-xie

thanks very much	多谢	duō-xiè
theatre	剧院	jù-yuàn
their	他们的	tā-men-de
there (over there)	那里	nà-lǐ
there is/there are	有	yǒu
there isn't.../ there aren't any...	没有…	méi yǒu...
these	这些	zhè-xiē
they	他们	tā-men
thief	小偷	xiǎo-tōu
third	第三	dì-sān
thirsty: *to be thirsty*	渴了	kě-le
thirteen	十三	shí-sān
thirty	三十	sān-shí
this	这个	zhè-ge
those	那些	nà-xiē
a thousand	一千	yī-qiān

three	三	sān
throat	喉咙	hóu-lóng
Thursday	星期四	xīng-qī-sì
ticket (bus, train, etc.)	车票	chē-piào
child ticket	儿童票	ér-tóng-piào
adult ticket	成人票	chéng-rén-piào
student ticket	学生票	xué-shēng-piào
ticket (single)	单程票	dān-chéng-piào
ticket (return)	往返票	wǎng-fǎn-piào
ticket office	售票处	shòu-piào-chù
tights	裤袜	kù-wà
time	时间	shí-jiān
at what time...?	什么时间…?	shén-me shí-jiān?
what time is it?	几点了?	jǐ-diǎn le?
timetable	时刻表	shí-kè-biǎo
to tip (waiter)	付小费	fù-xiǎo-fèi
tip (for service)	小费	xiǎo-fèi
tobacco	香烟	xiāng-yān

tobacconist's	香烟店	xiāng-yān-diàn
today	今天	jīn-tiān
toilet	厕所	cè-suǒ
tomato	西红柿	xī-hóng-shì
tomatoes (tin)	西红柿罐头	xī-hóng-shì guàn-tóu
tomorrow	明天	míng-tiān
tongue	舌头	shé-tou
tonight	今晚	jīn-wǎn
tooth	牙	yá
toothache	牙疼	yá-téng
toothbrush	牙刷	yá-shuā
toothpaste	牙膏	yá-gāo
tourist information	游客资讯	yóu-kè zī-xùn
toys	玩具	wán-jù
toy shop	玩具店	wán-jù-diàn
traffic lights	交通灯	jiāo-tōng-dēng
train	火车	huǒ-chē

trainers	运动鞋	yùn-dòng-xié
to translate	翻译	fān-yì
to travel	旅行	lǚ-xíng
travel agent's	旅行社	lǚ-xíng-shè
trousers	裤子	kù-zi
Tuesday	星期二	xīng-qī-èr
to turn off (light, etc.)	关	guān
to turn on (light, etc.)	开	kāi
twelve	十二	shí-èr
twenty	二十	èr-shí
two	二	èr
tyre	轮胎	lún-tāi

U

umbrella	雨伞	yǔ-sǎn
underground (metro)	地铁	dì-tiě
underground station	地铁站	dì-tiě-zhàn

underpants	内衣裤	nèi-yī-kù
to understand	明白	míng-bai
I don't understand	我不明白	wǒ bù míng-bai
do you understand?	你明白吗?	nǐ míng-bai ma?
United Kingdom	英国	yīng-guó
United States	美国	měi-guó
university	大学	dà-xué
unleaded	无铅汽油	wú-qián-qì-yóu
to unlock	开锁	kāi-suǒ
up	上	shàng
urgent	紧急	jǐn-jí
us	我们	wǒ-men
to use	使用	shǐ-yòng

V

vacancy (in hotel)	空房	kōng-fáng
vacation	度假	dù-jià

valid	有效的	yǒu-xiào-de
valuable	有价值的	yǒu-jià-zhí-de
value	价值	jià-zhí
vegan	纯素食者	chún-sù-shí-zhě
vegetables	蔬菜	shū-cài
vegetarian	素食者	sù-shí-zhě
video camera	录像机	lù-xiàng-jī
village	乡村	xiāng-cūn
vinegar	醋	cù
virus	病毒	bìng-dú
visa	签证	qiān-zhèng
to visit	走访	zǒu-fǎng
voice	声音	shēng-yīn
to vomit	呕吐	ǒu-tù

W

to wait (for)	等	děng
waiter/waitress	服务员	fú-wù-yuán

English – Mandarin

walk	步行	bù-xíng
wall	墙	qiáng
wallet	钱包	qián-bāo
to want	想	xiǎng
I want…	我想…	wǒ xiǎng…
we want…	我们想…	wǒ-men xiǎng…
warm	温暖的	wēn-nuǎn-de
to wash	洗	xǐ
washing machine	洗衣机	xǐ-yī-jī
wasp sting	黄蜂叮刺	huáng-fēng-dīng-cì
watch	手表	shǒu-biǎo
water	水	shuǐ
boiled water	开水	kāi-shuǐ
cold water	冷水	lěng-shuǐ
hot water	热水	rè-shuǐ
mineral water	矿泉水	kuàng-quán-shuǐ
non-drinking water	非饮用水	fēi- yǐn-yòng-shuǐ

sparkling (water)	有汽泡的	yǒu qì-pào-de
still (water)	无汽泡的	wú qì-pào-de
watermelon	西瓜	xī-guā
way in	入口	rù-kǒu
way out	出口	chū-kǒu
we	我们	wǒ-men
to wear	穿	chuān
weather	天气	tiān-qì
weather forecast	天气预报	tiān-qì yù-bào
wedding	婚礼	hūn-lǐ
Wednesday	星期三	xīng-qī-sān
week	星期	xīng-qīng
weekend	周末	zhōu-mò
weekly	每周	měi-zhōu
weekly magazine	周刊杂志	zhōu-kān-zá-zhì
welcome	欢迎	huān-yín
you're welcome!	不客气！	bù kè-qì!

west	西方	xī-fāng
what	什么	shén-me
what is it?	那是什么?	nà- shì shén-me?
what's your name?	你叫什么名字?	nǐ jiào shén-me míng-zi?
wheel	车轮	chē-lún
when	什么时候	shén-me shí-hòu
where	哪里	nǎ-li
where are you from?	你是哪里人?	nǐ shì nǎ-li rén?
where can I/we go...?	我/我们去哪儿可以…	wǒ/wǒ-men qù nǎr?
where is... ?	…在哪儿?	...zài nǎr?
which	哪一个	nǎ-yī-gè
whisky	威士忌酒	wēi-shì-jì-jiǔ
white	白色的	bái-sè-de
who	谁	shuí
whose: whose is it?	那是谁的?	nà-shì shuí-de?
why	为什么	wèi-shén-me

wife	妻子	qī-zi
to win	赢	yíng
wind	风	fēng
window	窗户	chuāng-hù
windscreen	挡风玻璃	dǎng-fēng-bō-li
windscreen washer	挡风玻璃清洗器	dǎng-fēng-bō-li-qīng-xǐ-qì
windscreen wiper	挡风玻璃刮水器	dǎng-fēng-bō-li-guā-shuǐ-qì
wine	葡萄酒	pú-táo-jiǔ
red wine	红葡萄酒	hóng pú-táo-jiǔ
white wine	白葡萄酒	bái pú-táo-jiǔ
winter	冬天	dōng-tiān
with	和/加	hé/jiā
with a double bed	有双人床	yǒu shuāng-rén-chuáng
with bath	有浴缸	yǒu yù-gāng
with ice	加冰	jiā-bīng
with lemon	加柠檬	jiā níng-méng

English – Mandarin

with milk	加奶	jiā-nǎi
with shower	有淋浴	yǒu lín-yù
with sugar	加糖	jiā-táng
without	不加	bù-jiā
without ice	不加冰	bù-jiā bīng
without milk	不加奶	bù-jiā nǎi
without sugar	不加糖	bù-jiā táng
wok	炒菜锅	chǎo-cài-gūo
woman	女士	nǚ-shì
work	工作	gōng-zuò
world	世界	shì-jiè
write: *please write it down*	请把它写下来	qǐng bǎ tā xiě-xià-lái
wrong	错	cuò

X

x-ray	X光	x-guāng
to x-ray	照X光	zhào x-guāng

Y

year	年	nián
last year	去年	qù-nián
next year	明年	míng-nián
this year	今年	jīn-nián
yellow	黄色的	huáng-sè-de
yes	是	shì
yes, please	好, 谢谢	hǎo, xiè-xie
yesterday	昨天	zuó-tiān
yet: not yet	还没有	hái-méi-yǒu
yoghurt	酸奶	suān-nǎi
you	你/你们	nǐ/nǐ-men
and you?	你呢?	nǐ ne?
young	年轻的	nián-qīng-de
your	你的/你们的	nǐ-de/nǐ-men-de

Z

| zone | 区域 | qū-yù |
| zoo | 动物园 | dòng-wù-yuán |